# THE EASTER PROCLAMATION 1916
*A Comparative Analysis*

# THE
# EASTER PROCLAMATION 1916

## *A Comparative Analysis*

Liam de Paor

*with an essay by W.J. Mc Cormack*

FOUR COURTS PRESS
*in association with the*
IRISH LABOUR PARTY

Set in 11 on 14 point Bembo for
FOUR COURTS PRESS LTD
7 Malpas Street, Dublin 8, Ireland
www.fourcourtspress.ie
and in North America by
FOUR COURTS PRESS
c/o ISBS, 920 N.E. 58th Avenue, Suite 300, Portland, OR 97213.

First edition 1997
Second edition 2016

ISBN 978-1-84682-619-1

A catalogue record for this title
is available from the British Library.

Support for this publication was received from the Irish Labour Party,
Ciaran Brady, Carla King, Willie and Therese Nolan, and Pat Rabbitte.

Printed in England
by CPI Antony Rowe, Chippenham, Wilts.

For Kathleen and Domhnall

# Contents

# POBLACHT NA H EIREANN.

## THE PROVISIONAL GOVERNMENT
### OF THE
# IRISH REPUBLIC
## TO THE PEOPLE OF IRELAND.

IRISHMEN AND IRISHWOMEN : In the name of God and of the dead generations from which she receives her old tradition of nationhood, Ireland, through us, summons her children to her flag and strikes for her freedom.

Having organised and trained her manhood through her secret revolutionary organisation, the Irish Republican Brotherhood, and through her open military organisations, the Irish Volunteers and the Irish Citizen Army, having patiently perfected her discipline, having resolutely waited for the right moment to reveal itself, she now seizes that moment, and, supported by her exiled children in America and by gallant allies in Europe, but relying in the first on her own strength, she strikes in full confidence of victory.

We declare the right of the people of Ireland to the ownership of Ireland, and to the unfettered control of Irish destinies, to be sovereign and indefeasible. The long usurpation of that right by a foreign people and government has not extinguished the right, nor can it ever be extinguished except by the destruction of the Irish people. In every generation the Irish people have asserted their right to national freedom and sovereignty : six times during the past three hundred years they have asserted it in arms. Standing on that fundamental right and again asserting it in arms in the face of the world, we hereby proclaim the Irish Republic as a Sovereign Independent State, and we pledge our lives and the lives of our comrades-in-arms to the cause of its freedom, of its welfare, and of its exaltation among the nations.

The Irish Republic is entitled to, and hereby claims, the allegiance of every Irishman and Irishwoman. The Republic guarantees religious and civil liberty, equal rights and equal opportunities to all its citizens, and declares its resolve to pursue the happiness and prosperity of the whole nation and of all its parts, cherishing all the children of the nation equally, and oblivious of the differences carefully fostered by an alien government, which have divided a minority from the majority in the past.

Until our arms have brought the opportune moment for the establishment of a permanent National Government, representative of the whole people of Ireland and elected by the suffrages of all her men and women, the Provisional Government, hereby constituted, will administer the civil and military affairs of the Republic in trust for the people.

We place the cause of the Irish Republic under the protection of the Most High God, Whose blessing we invoke upon our arms, and we pray that no one who serves that cause will dishonour it by cowardice, inhumanity, or rapine. In this supreme hour the Irish nation must, by its valour and discipline and by the readiness of its children to sacrifice themselves for the common good, prove itself worthy of the august destiny to which it is called.

Signed on Behalf of the Provisional Government,

THOMAS J. CLARKE,
SEAN Mac DIARMADA,     THOMAS MacDONAGH,
P. H. PEARSE,     EAMONN CEANNT,
JAMES CONNOLLY.     JOSEPH PLUNKETT.

# Introduction

W.J. McCORMACK

## I: MY FRIEND, THE AUTHOR

The historian and political thinker Liam de Paor (1926–98) was a radical, in the sense that, as he grew, he adapted. It was therefore not wholly surprising that coverage of his death in the *Irish Times* gave three distinct accounts of him. The first stressed originality as a political thinker, a preference for Irish independence over Irish unity. The second dwelt on commitments to Gaelic culture in both scholarly and colloquial terms. The third, by a professional archaeologist, mixed tributes to de Paor's learning with heartfelt acknowledgments of his modesty and his humour.

De Paor's immediate family background lay in east Munster, Waterford to be precise. His father, who worked for the railways in pre-independent Ireland, found himself beached in Dublin at the time of the Easter Rising. He stayed on, married and started a family. Liam was born ten years later, on 13 April 1926. In the same year Sean O'Casey's *The Plough and the Stars* outraged citizens of the new state with its irreverent, tragi-comic view of nationalist politics. This was a fitting moment for the author of an incisive yet sympathetic analysis of the 1916 Proclamation to slip on to the stage of left-wing affairs. While he never shouted from the rooftops, his was not a mute role; he was never a spear carrier.

His emergence as a political thinker was slow. He trained initially as an architect in University College, Dublin. His contemporaries included Liam Miller (another architect who changed course to pioneer literary publishing in post-war Ireland), Anthony Cronin (a barrister, but best known as a writer) and Charles J. Haughey (an accountant turned politician and tax-cheat). Changing direction signified much for this generation.

Partly at least through the influence of his first wife, Máire McDermott (an art historian from Co. Derry), de Paor abandoned architecture for archaeology. His knowledge of buildings as things to be designed and built in the present greatly assisted his work on the surviving structures of antiquity. Their joint work, *Early Christian Ireland* (1958), published in the Thames and Hudson series and often reprinted, contributed to the growing public awareness of early Irish history, which profoundly affected issues of ethnicity and identity in the troubled decades to come. These issues, in turn, preoccupied him, not so much for their alleged weighty substance as for the dark shadows they still cast as ideological concepts today.

De Paor did not fit the stay-at-Home-Rule UCD mould. He worked in 1945 as a draughtsman in Harry Clarke's stained-glass studios, and in the sixties served UNESCO in Nepal as an advisor. During his years (1965–86) on the staff of UCD, he lectured in American history as well as his own more obvious specialisms. He was an eloquent and charming speaker of Gaelic, who participated regularly in those learned bacchanalian summer schools honouring the poet Brian Merriman (fl. 1780). In the 1960s and after, he was a regular contributor to *Comhar*. One of de Paor's last publications was an English-language translation (published in the journal *Times Change*) of a lecture he had first given at Merriman in Gaelic.

De Paor was well known as an excavating archaeologist. Indeed, he was 'on a dig' in the midlands when news broke of serious trouble in Ulster in August 1969. His immediate response was to volunteer assistance in whatever form he could to the expected flow of refugees from the Catholic quarters of Belfast. In the course of heady consultations, he was asked if his professional travels abroad might provide cover for an importation of arms. His firm answer was in the negative, not only—as he repeated the matter to me the year before he died—because he did not believe arms would help the situation, but because he profoundly distrusted the persons in Fianna Fáil who made the approach. On television, he made this episode public, repeating his specification of Fianna Fáil as the ideological stable to which the tempters were attached.

His more lasting response to the recurrence of violence in 1969 was *Divided Ulster* (1970), commissioned by Penguin Books as one of the first of their 'specials' on the Irish Troubles.[1] Although it is essentially a historical study, it indicates clearly its author's acute political sense. De Paor had joined the Labour Party before the fashionable influx of seeming left-wingers—Conor Cruise O'Brien, David Thornley and (less seeming) Justin Keating—

---

1 Other publications on the same topic include T.W. Moody, *The Ulster Question, 1603–1973* (Dublin: Cork: Mercier, 1974) and Owen Dudley Edwards, *The Sins of Our Fathers: Roots of Conflict in Northern Ireland* (Dublin: Gill and Macmillan, 1970).

which swept it into a coalition government with Fine Gael in 1973. De Paor attended meetings of the Sean Connolly Branch in Dublin's south-east constituency, an eccentric coterie not least in its choice of venue—a café of the vegetarian tendency frequented by Christine, Lady Longford (novelist), O.Z. Whitehead (Baha'i actor) and sundry Trotskyites with their Special Branch shadows. At all times, de Paor remained a rock of sense when Labour members met these luminaries before or after party meetings, courteous, insistent on procedure and principle, quietly mischievous.

A Russian translation of *Divided Ulster* was published in Moscow in 1974, the Soviets' tacit recognition of (Official) Sinn Féin and its faltering military wing. None of this was to de Paor's liking. Even when Fine Gael changed leader and Garret FitzGerald initiated a social-democratic renewal of his party, de Paor continued to oppose coalition as an option for Labour. His interests were so diverse that few thought of him as a political thinker, though he was sought-after as a commentator on radio and television. A column, 'Roots', published in the *Irish Times*, provided an opportunity not only to broadcast his opinions but also to test and modify them.

After he retired from UCD in 1986, de Paor spent much time in America. He separated from his first wife and, three years after her death in 1994, married Deirdre Glenn. Few of the many friends who called to their flat in Dartry realised that he had passed three score and ten; he continued to work incessantly, publishing new material on Saint Patrick and (separately) on contemporary politics. There was also a long paper on the poet Thomas Moore (1779–1852).

A book title of 1990 summarises the loss felt by many in Ireland and elsewhere when on the day of the Omagh bombing, de Paor was cremated in Dublin—*Unfinished Business*. Ten years earlier, the title would have been glossed as a republican manifesto. However, de Paor's evolving political thought radically challenged the dogmas of Irish republicanism, especially the easy assumption that differences were mergeable in some comprehensive notion of Irishness. Though he remained faithful to the Labour Party, his influence was discernible in Democratic Left (in whose journal he published his last article) and even in Fine Gael, for whom he never held out much hope.

At the time of his death, I wrote that Liam de Paor was not to be remembered as part of some professional cadre of Irish political scientists (Basil Chubb, Brian Farrell et al.). As a passionate dissident his name would be found among names more lovingly honoured than loudly celebrated. In the company of Fred Ryan, Louie Bennett, Father Francis Shaw, Seán Mac Reamoinn and Jimmy Kemmy, Liam de Paor would feel at home, having earned a good rest. There would be lively talk everywhere, and not a dry tongue in Liam's corner of the heavenly mansions.


II: DIVIDED ULSTER

*On the Easter Proclamation and Other Declarations* (1997) was one of de Paor's last books, followed only by *Landscapes with Figures: People, Culture and Art in Ireland and the Modern World* (1998)—the contrast of titles is characteristic of the author. It is regrettably short but, for compensation, detailed, highly original and animated with a recurrent impatience. Its first part is devoted to a comparative tracing of sources of influence, including the American Declaration of Independence (1776) and the French Declaration of the Rights of Man (1789), while the second, more closely argued part invokes a variety of individuals, including Martin Luther and Abraham Lincoln, as it proceeds to analyse the Proclamation's six paragraphs and its prefatory headings. As a single (unsigned) blurb-like page stated, 'This is an essay on words.'

By this terse yet undramatic statement, *On the Easter Proclamation* marks itself off from *Divided Ulster*. The earlier book, written in urgent response to a tumultuous (and soon very violent) crisis, was unashamedly the work of an Irish nationalist historian. He was distinguished from most of that kind by his labour-socialist views and by his familiarity with political figures, events and locations inside Northern Ireland. Intimate knowledge of 'British Occupied Ireland' was not a *sine qua non* when it came to pontificating. De Paor's tone was elegantly low key, but penetrating. He wrote out of a tradition that regarded Irish independence and the political unity of the island as self-evidently just objectives, though he was not blind to the shortcomings of the southern republic.

In 1970, it was inevitable that a rapidly prepared book about contemporary Northern Ireland would focus on events, incidents, marches, attacks, deaths. While *Divided Ulster* provided a thorough historical perspective on the recent troubles, it did not enjoy the luxury of abstract reflection. His access to Penguin was eased by an earlier publication under the same imprint, *Archaeology: an Illustrated Introduction* (1967), evidence of a non-insular mind. Thirty years later, in 1997, *On the Easter Proclamation* addressed what one can only call a multiple history. There had been decades of terror and counter-terror; eighty years had passed since the Proclamation had been first read and derided, then digested and sanctified. And there was the longer history an archaeologist could draw on—for example—to imagine a pre-Norman, or even pre-Christian society in which neither Catholic nor Protestant raised hackles.

The twin vocations as historian of the non-recent past and current affairs analyst collaborated effectively. In December 1970, de Paor published a column in the *Irish Times*, in which he advised that we would not:

> learn a great deal about the origins of the political culture of Ulster by studying the seventeenth-century plantations (although we will learn something). But by studying the myth and saga into which seventeenth-century history has been transmuted in the traditions of the North, we may learn a great deal about the present-day political culture.[2]

Less compactly, he advises that we should attend to the transmission of beliefs about the past, and the evidences of transmission. For an example take the many republications of John Temple's highly partisan and self-interested *History of the Irish Rebellion of 1641, together with the Barbarous Cruelties and Bloody Massacres that ensued thereupon* (first published 1646) reaching to the end of the eighteenth century when it was overtaken by the United Irishmen's very different enterprise.

The Easter Proclamation contributed its own mite to this process. Consider Paragraph 3, 'In every generation the Irish people have asserted their right to national freedom and sovereignty; six times during the past three hundred years, they have asserted it in arms.' Efforts to tally these six rebellions have proved awkward; if we work back from 1916 [1] through the Fenian risings of 1867 [2], Emmet's Dublin insurrection [3], the United Irishmen of Connacht, Leinster and Ulster [4], the Jacobite resistance to the new King William III in 1688–91 [5], then we require the insurrection of October 1641, an essentially royalist uprising (with local score settling encouraged) to count as [6]. This last-mentioned had nothing to do with sovereignty (except that of a sovereign monarch), separatism, nationalism or indeed 'freedom' as Pearse and Connolly understood the term. De Paor

---

2 'Ulster's Two Cultures in Poetry', *Irish Times*, 3 December 1970, p. 10.

refers to this recitation as Pearse's 'schematic myth'. He carefully notes that, in the late 1640s, 'the Confederate Catholics at Kilkenny had put forward the case that Ireland was a distinct and separate kingdom under the Stuart Crown'. However, 'that is not quite the same thing'—de Paor's mild rebuke—as the justification claimed by the Proclamation's emphasis on sovereignty and independence.

As author of an essay on words—480 or so words—he was well able to draw upon Irish history of those centuries implied in the 1916 text, and did so in a manner not always flattering to a supposed foundational document of the present Republic of Ireland. His professional training related to earlier centuries, to early Christian and pre-Christian Ireland. His sardonic commentary on the signatories' lack of a Gaelic word for 'republic' is the only significant point at which his linguistic capacity is mobilised. (The issue complicated a meeting between Eamon de Valera and Lloyd George in July 1921, when the UK prime minister, a Welshman, observed that the Celts did not appear to have a concept of republic.)

Máire de Paor wrote pithily on the issue of terminology in reviewing *The Celtic Consciousness* (ed. Robert O'Driscoll) in 1982. Noting many misapplications, from lush tales of Lancelot and Guinevere to spurious ideas of race, she insisted Celtic 'is essentially a linguistic term'.[3] The book she reviewed, reproducing papers delivered at a Toronto conference, 'has the same very broad, not to say indiscriminate, definition of what is "Celtic"'. Two strands within the Canadian proceedings can be identified, the first scholarly to the nth degree, the second contentious. Heinrich Wagner argued that Africa provided important non-Indo-European elements to the Celtic languages, while the poet John Montague and Conor Cruise-O'Brien argued about contemporary Ulster. Mrs de Paor preferred Montague, a fellow northerner.

The long *durée* from the earliest pre-Celtic human habitations to the helter-Celtic cannot easily be traced through a single continuum of transmissions. The pre-Celtic is the archaeologists' domain, where linguistic evidence is non-existent. Other semiotic codes have been identified in the material culture—solar alignments in tombs, incised figures (circles, lozenges, spirals) on buried stones, the arrangement of hearths and middens. Mid-twentieth-century archaeology was actively engaged with this material, quickly adopting new technological devices and methods. A

---

**3** *Irish Times*, 16 October 1982, p. 12.

significant debate arose about the coastal landing place of the first Neolithic settlers—the Boyne Valley *versus* Sligo Bay.

A fuller knowledge of pre-Celtic Ireland would not tell us much about modern Ireland, its inhabitants, their culture, their social habits. But—to apply de Paor's dictum about the plantations—to study how modern Ireland has responded to, or has applied, what is known of that past might tell us a great deal. For example, the rival locations established for the first megalithic incursion *taken together* fairly closely mark the western and eastern termini of the partitioning border dividing Northern Ireland from the Free State in 1922 (and ever since).

## III: A DIGRESSION THROUGH ESTYN EVANS

In 1961, a Dutch historical geographer, Marcus Willem Heslinga (1922–2009), published a complex study, *The Irish Border as a Cultural Divide*, fulfilling the University of Utrecht's requirements for a doctoral degree. Several editions have followed, the most recent in 2000. His argument did not reach back to the Neolithic period but pointed to the Black Pig's Dyke, a system of earthen embankments built around the time of the Celtic invasion along a line from Donegal Bay to Carlingford Lough, as essentially an Ulster-defensive construction. To entertain the notion (and Heslinga clearly did) that the dyke 'follows the border of the United Kingdom', is surely to put the cart before the Black Pig.[4] Through his quiet career he taught in the Free University of Amsterdam, a confessional neo-Calvinist institution founded in 1879.

For obvious reasons, Heslinga's acknowledgments are predominantly Dutch; among relatively few Irish (or Irish-based) names, the only academic authority mentioned is Emyr Estyn Evans (1905–89), first and long-reigning professor of geography at the Queen's University Belfast. In many ways this is an unremarkable emphasis; Queen's had the oldest geography department on the island of Ireland. Evans had arrived as a lecturer in 1928, auspiciously supported. Happily for Heslinga, the Welshman became a vigorous practitioner of historical geography. A hardbound issue of Heslinga's study carried a two-page foreword by Evans

---

**4** M.W. Heslinga, *The Irish Border as a Cultural Divide: a Contribution to the Study of Regionalism in the British Isles* (Assen: van Gorcum, 1962), pp 110–11.

who was 'personally grateful' to his Dutch student for taking on the task of elucidating Irish partition to a wider world. The foreword had begun in mock-oracular style—'of the histories of Irish Partition there is no end', referring to a body of mainly nationalist complaints, with fewer unionist vindications issued from 1920 onwards, that is, following the practical and legally approved establishment of a border. Heslinga's distinction for Evans was to write history as a human geographer.

Evans, like the de Paors, had a *longue durée* view of matters. He was brusquely dismissive of any racial theorising, and poured mild scorn on notions of 'the historic Irish nation', mentioning in the same breadth however 'a politically independent Ulster'; independent, that is, from the rest of the island. He does not enunciate a proto-historic demarcation of the northern province (or region); his focus is more urgent. There then follow conventional nostrums on southern ironies including its attachment to a Catholic church which had condemned disloyalty and 'militant action', but more enviously noting its celebrated literary eloquence in the English language, 'whereas the taciturn North gets a poor press'.

De Paor's 'Roots' article of December 1970, quoted above, arose from a Northern Irish Arts Council project to address the divisions of Ulster by sending a pair of writers—one Catholic (John Montague), the other Protestant (John Hewitt)—on tour of the province, reading poems together that reflected their different histories. Hewitt's reputation as a 'man of the left' had long incorporated a strong interest in regionalism as a means to overcoming contemporary divisions, and in his pursuit of this he had reviewed several of Evans's books. The notice of *Irish Heritage* (1942), appearing in *The Bell*, did not entirely please Evans, who commented, 'I feel you have taken the meat out very adroitly'.[5] Hewitt never published an extensive account of his regionalist ideas, though articles appeared in the *Ulster Young Farmer* and other front-line outposts. His name nowhere appears in Heslinga's *Contribution to a Study of Regionalism in the British Isles* or its bibliography. When the great crisis of Hewitt's life as an art-gallery curator came in 1952 with his being passed over for the directorship of Belfast's civic museum by a political cabal, his acutely observant wife wrote in her journal, 'Professor Evans is somewhere in it.'[6]

---

**5** See W.J. Mc Cormack, *Northman: John Hewitt (1907–1987). An Irish Writer, His World and His Times* (Oxford: Oxford University Press, 2015), p. 95.   **6** Mc Cormack, *Northman*, p. 141.

Certainly the Welsh professor of geography spread himself widely. The online *Dictionary of Welsh Biography* sketches the implications with a light touch. 'Evans's academic interests [had] focussed initially on relationships between prehistoric and proto-historic communities and their natural environment.' Much later in his Belfast career, 'from an increasingly profound understanding of Ireland's prehistory, it seemed to him a short, inevitable step to attempt recovery of its rapidly disappearing peasant culture and folklore'.[7] Quite what recovery might mean is left un-glossed. Behind the problematic short step lay a rich engagement through field work, excavation, other forms of research, and numerous publications. Yet, in another light, the supposition of an *inevitable* step is not categorically astray from a definition of the word 'Irish' offered by one of Heslinga's lesser authorities. By it, Desmond Fennell emphatically meant 'the oldest and truest Irish, the present carrier-group of Irish destiny—the Irish Catholic peasantry, whether living in the cities, towns or countryside'.[8] Or in equation form: Oldest = Truest = Present Carrier of Destiny. One should not assume that Heslinga accepted this nonsense, but its inscription in his programmatic account of Irish cultural divisions deserves recovery.

Heslinga visited Ireland, north and south, in 1959, 1960 and 1961. He took little interest in contemporary social conditions—cultural apathy, rural poverty, sluggish economic activity, emigration. He did pick up the 'two nations' theory and noted 'hundreds of acts of violence' along the border over a five- or six-year period, seemingly a unique phenomenon in Western Europe.[9] The IRA's border campaign was called off one month before *The Irish Border as a Cultural Divide* was published. The recent carrier-group of Irish destiny had, in effect, stood itself down. Evans's best-known publication, *Irish Heritage* (1st ed. March 1942), was then twenty years old, the product of labours conducted under wartime conditions. In its final pages, he dwelt on the untraceably long practice of folk traditions; for example, every major process of the farmer's year has or had its associated or appropriate rites 'which clung to them *from the beginning*' [emphasis added]. This beginning (the next paragraph tells us) occurred in the Mediterranean region 'where the megalithic religion took

---

**7** Both quoted sentences are taken from Llandre Colin Thomas's entry in the (online) *Dictionary of Welsh Biography*.  **8** Heslinga, op. cit., p. 81b. The authority was Desmond Fennell (born 1929 in Belfast), briefly an editor on an English language *Collected Correspondence* of Johann Herder, and controversialist.  **9** Heslinga, p. 9.

its rise', circa 3000 BC.[10] I do not doubt the acumen Evans brought to the matter, but nothing like a verifiable line of transmission to the holy wells of Tyrone is on offer.

Why does this matter in a tribute republication of *On the Easter Proclamation*? Summarising the outcome of the 1885 general election and Gladstone's newly proclaimed objective of Home Rule for Ireland, de Paor judged that 'Ulster was therefore divided almost evenly, and the division of Ulster divided Ireland.'[11] On the forces immediately at play, he noted that a crucial factor had been the social radicalism of Michael Davitt, who ultimately wanted land nationalisation and not just tenant ownership. In a long schematic myth of Ireland as immemorially divided along the line over-determined through lists of drumlin locations, mega-lith-tomb sites, Jacobean settlements, and later party-fights, Davitt's social radicalism was trumped. The schematism emerged after partition and long after the death of land nationalisation dreams; it emerged notably through Heslinga's dissertation, supervised in Utrecht but overseen (perhaps directed) by Professor Evans.

The formidable resulting argument was a little shaken by *Divided Ulster*, especially by de Paor's adroit documentation of electoral gerrymandering, police sectarianism and bad faith in high places. The book's appearance under the Penguin imprint gave it added authority outside Ireland. Senior members of the British Labour Party and responsible politicians in Washington took note. The sense of permanence that the Heslinga thesis exuded can now be analysed as depending in part on the deployment of partisan nationalist-republican material which did more to discredit the argument against permanent partition than to strengthen it—Frank Curran's *Irish Fascist City* (1946), Desmond Fennell's *The Northern Catholic*

10 E. Estyn Evans, *Irish Heritage: the Landscape, the People and their Work* (1st ed. 1942, Dundalk: Tempest, 1977, p. 163). In the penultimate chapter he writes, 'the megalithic tra-dition in which so many of the Elder Faiths are rooted took firm hold on the Mourne country fifty centuries ago', though he admits that the arrival of the potato from the New World and 'periodic waves of refugees washed up into the hills by tides of sectarian strife' have had some influence (see 4th ed. 1989, p. 203). In *Unfinished Business* (London: Hutchinson, 1990), de Paor quotes (p. 108) Evans declaring 'I'm a pagan, quite frankly', but proceeds to examine 'unreconstructed seventeenth-century fundamentalism' in parts of Co. Down and notes 'more numerous small groups derived from Evangelical enthusi-asms generated by the dislocations and disorientations caused by nineteenth-century indus-trialization, or by the subsequent failures of industries'. 11 Liam de Paor, *Divided Ulster* (2nd ed., London: Penguin, 1971), p. 57.

(1958) and Sean MacBride's *Our People, Our Money* (1949). The Ulster (Catholic) novelist Benedict Kiely's *Counties of Contention* (1945), with its plea for compromise and amity, was not cited.

Evans's pagan declaration appeared in *Ulster: the Common Ground*, a pamphlet of 1984 reprinted in a posthumous collection though without the paganism.[12] Some pages later, one finds a very brief note on Adolf Mahr, an Austrian archaeologist whom de Valera appointed director of the National Museum of Ireland in 1934. Evans recounts how he discovered Mahr's Nazi commitments and the extent of his spying in Ireland as archaeological surveyor. He had quietly disappeared from the National Museum with the outbreak of war, and his office lay respectfully unmolested virtually till the cessation of hostilities. De Paor told me that, once broken open by staff members, it was found to contain radio transmitters and other gadgets of treachery. I am not aware that de Valera, whose son was a megalithic specialist in UCD—and de Paor's boss—ever apologised to the Irish people for his error of judgment. Somewhere among Liam's effects, there may be found a copy of the German plan for cultural administration, passed to him by Desmond Williams; apart from Evans, others marked for positions of authority were Joseph Raftery and Ada Longfield.

Politics and archaeology certainly enjoyed a curious intimacy in Ireland throughout the twentieth century, some of it deriving from romantic antiquarianism and local pride. The repressive censorship that grew rapidly in the Free State and its successor was satirically evaded by some novelists, including Austin Clarke and Mervyn Wall who, for contrast, evoked the pre-Norman and non-Roman church of the Irish Celts. De Paor did not respond to the challenge of poeticised archaeology by proclaiming a truly scientific alternative, but by evolving a critical perspective that reached its apogee in his analysis of the Easter Proclamation.

Evans's appointment in Belfast certainly was no error of judgment comparable to Dublin's embrace of Mahr; he settled in for a long and loyal career that ended only with his death in 1989. His widow's memoir helpfully details the earliest stages—an interview on 29 May 1928 (his twenty-third birthday), and a subsequent meeting (somewhere in Britain, probably London) with Thomas Jones.[13] 'Benefiting from some insights

**12** E. Estyn Evans, *Ireland and the Atlantic Heritage: Selected Writings* (Dublin: Lilliput, 1996), p. 164.   **13** Gwynneth Evans, 'Estyn: a Biographical Memoir' in Evans, *Ireland and the Atlantic Heritage*, pp 2, 5.

given by Dr Thomas Jones CH, Evans was appointed lecturer in Geography at The Queen's University, Belfast, with responsibility for establishing a new department.'[14] This was an astonishing achievement in a young man of impoverished background, suspect health, much interrupted education and no experience; and it carried awesome responsibilities from the outset. Who caused it all to happen thus?

In 1909, Jones had been appointed the first professor of economics at Queen's, but departed after two years. On this basis his knowledge of the university would have been comparatively slight, and made slighter by the passage of close on twenty years. By 1928, however, Jones was Deputy Secretary to the British Cabinet, having served Lloyd George in that capacity during the Anglo-Irish negotiations. Indeed, while de Valera had struggled to find a Gaelic word for republic, Jones and the PM had chatted between themselves in Welsh. During the treaty discussions of 1921, it was Jones who persuaded Arthur Griffith to accept a boundary commission. While one could rhapsodise on the question of political influence, and the significance of linking the new geography department to that of economics in the Faculty of Commerce, it may—in the *longue durée*—make more sense to note the shared Calvinist upbringing of Estyn Evans, Thomas Jones and M.W. Heslinga. What is predestination but an exaggerated *durée*—God foreseen and God forsaken, as Pascal might have remarked had he known the immense silent valleys of the Mourne country?

IV: LIAM DE PAOR'S CRITIQUE

Mini-histories of Thomas Jones and Estyn Evans in Belfast and Eamon de Valera and Adolf Mahr in Dublin, *taken together*, go some way towards demonstrating dangerous intersections of politics and archaeology (or historical geography) that can result from arrogant or negligent route-planning. Liam de Paor was alert to the risk of collisions, not least from his experience of Fianna Fáil blandishments. If *Divided Ulster* (1970) retained traces of the elder nationalist faith, these were considerably reduced by 1990. Having opened *Unfinished Business* declaring that 'the great problems of our contemporary world are moral', de Paor proceeded with Karl W. Deutsch's definition of a nation—'a group of persons united by a common

14 See *Dictionary of Welsh Biography*, loc. cit.

error and a common dislike of their neighbours'.[15] Pursuing this trajectory we come to *On the Easter Proclamation* (1997).

The document issued on 24 April 1916 is remarkable for the near-unanimity with which it has been approved by later generations. Understandably brief—486 words by de Paor's count—it has contributed some memorable phrases to the general lexicon of Irish political debate. The opening invocation of God has pleased the traditionalists. The explicit inclusion of Irish *women* has won the approval of feminists and other radicals, while also boosting an apprehension of the Proclamation's elusive democratic character. 'Cherishing all the children of the nation equally' is the most frequently cited phrase even if, from time to time, differences have arisen about what group or groups are referred to.

Maybe popularity has obstructed any extended examination of the Easter Proclamation. De Paor's long essay of 1997 is the only detailed and sustained account I am aware of, scandalously left out of print during the exhausting run-up to the centenary year.[16] Perhaps the centennial committees might provide an explanation of their (we presume) *studied* neglect of it. What I want to attempt here is a brief appendix (more accurately, prefix) to his argument. He offers (in the first part) comparisons with other declarations Irish, French and American, and (in the second) analyses of the text that include a search of the signatories' individual contributions or influence. Where Liam had focused on American and French declarations of the eighteenth century, I will refer passingly to contemporary French influences, involving Georges Sorel (1847–1922) and Henri Bergson (1859–1941), also an English Fabian trace. Finally, I attempt to identify a specific point in the Proclamation where Connolly's syndicalism can be excavated. This is not to suggest some inadequacy in de Paor's work, but to complement his account of historical contexts—the American and French revolutions, the Fenian movement etc.—through influences more directly contemporary with the makers of the 1916 insurrection.

For the sake of economy I concentrate on two separate sentences. My first is taken from near the middle of Paragraph 3, the longest in the Proclamation. Having a little shakily asserted a certain right or rights of the Irish people to be 'sovereign and indefeasible', the signatories continue—

---

15 Liam de Paor, *Unfinished Business: Ireland Today and Tomorrow* (London: Hutchinson, 1990), pp 1, 5.  16 Liam de Paor, *On the Easter Proclamation and Other Declarations* (Dublin: Four Courts Press, 1997).

'The long usurpation of that right by a foreign people and government has not extinguished the right, nor can it ever be extinguished except by the destruction of the Irish people.' The repetition of 'people' underlines a broad nineteenth-century understanding of nationalism not in itself contentious here. But 'the destruction of the Irish people' strikes two discordant notes at once—one, the physical destruction of the people; and, two, the destruction of an Irishness forever awaiting an accepted definition.

Questions of what has become known in the mid-twentieth century as genocide do arise about specific limited periods of Irish history, principally the Elizabethan conquest in its late phase, and the Cromwellian campaign of the 1640s. But nothing like physical extinction was attempted nor was it possible. The huge toll of lives caused by the famine of 1845 onwards was retrospectively assigned by nationalists to British responsibility, though the famine itself had multiple causes. The feared destruction of *Irishness* was not without a grim prehistory, but it became a preoccupation of the late Victorian period and after. Douglas Hyde's lecture-pamphlet, *On the Necessity for De-Anglicising Ireland* (1892), opened by making an unsustainable distinction: 'we mean it, not as a protest against imitating what is best in the English people, for that would be absurd, but rather to show the folly of neglecting what is Irish, and hastening to adopt, pell-mell, and indiscriminately, everything that is English, simply because it is English.'[17] The concession—that 'what is best in the English people' had validity—was quickly opposed, in practical affairs by the policy of Sinn Féin, and more eloquently in the writings of Patrick Pearse, which de Paor examines closely (see Index below). D.P. Moran railed against 'national degeneration' and 'the obliteration of the Irish nation', longing for nothing less than 'the battle of two civilisations' to reverse the trend.[18] Among the signatories, Sean MacDermott was especially sensitive to what he believed to be a master plan to anglicise Ireland, and his attitude towards socialism reflected that suspicion, 'we are sick of the international democrat who has little effect on Ireland except to further anglicise the country.'[19] Pearse's fear that his generation would fail to rebel discloses more clearly the connections between the psychology of ethno-

---

17 Hyde, www.thefuture.ie/the-necessity ...   18 D.P. Moran, *The Philosophy of Irish Ireland*, ed. Patrick Maume (Dublin: UCD Press, 2006), pp 7, 23, 94–114.   19 Quoted in Gerard MacAtasney, *Seán MacDiarmada: the Mind of the Revolution* (Manorhamilton: Drumlin Publications, 2004), p. 155.

nationalism and the widespread sense of degeneration or degeneracy encouraged by Max Nordau and other systematic cultural pessimists.

My second chosen sentence constitutes the Proclamation's second to last paragraph. It reads:

> Until our arms have brought the opportune moment for the establish-ment of a permanent National Government, representative of the whole people of Ireland and elected by the suffrages of all her men and women, the Provisional Government, hereby constituted, will admin-ister the civil and military affairs of the Republic in trust for the people.

The implications are extensive. The first point to be noted is its objec-tive, arrangements for the establishment of a national government. There is no suggestion of an elected assembly or anything anticipating the Dáil Éireann set up in January 1919. Consequently, one can draw no conclu-sions about the presence or inclusion of persons critical of or opposed to the Provisional Government. All of this was, of course, intended to pro-ceed from the *success* of armed rebellion: a situation in which—to choose a few possible candidates—neither the pacifist Frank Sheehy Skeffington nor the Volunteers' chief Eoin MacNeill could hope to find a place. Nor would the 100,000 or so unionist male voters in the December 1910 elec-tions (nineteen constituencies), and the hardly fewer supporters of unop-posed unionist candidates in ten other constituencies. The Proclamation was partitionist by default.

The inclusion of women among prospective voters in the unlikely election gave evidence of an intended practical implementation of the gender equality announced earlier. It also acknowledged the positive influence of Cumann na mBan and the Citizen Army's women members. However, the largest demonstration of women's political commitment in these years had come through the Ulster Covenant of September 1912, when more than 230,000 women from the northern province had signed their declaration of support, only fractionally fewer than the male signa-tories of the blood-Covenant itself. De Paor mischievously quotes the Covenant to demonstrate the Proclamation's echoing of it and, in a foot-note, lists the nineteen members of the Ulster Provisional Government of whom fifteen were MPs elected or unopposed (see p. 120, n23 below).

No one can complain about the omission of details about suffrage qualifications in a document of such brevity. The avoidance of any reference to an elected assembly, indeed to an assembly of any kind, is more significant. For those in the know, it conformed to a long-standing Fenian distrust of parliaments and of representative politics generally. Yet it is difficult to see how a National Government, chosen directly, could in any way satisfy 'the whole people of Ireland'—unless, of course, all non-nationalist men and women were excluded from everything.

At the Second International's Congress in Zurich in August 1893, direct democracy or direct election, as against parliamentarianism, got on the agenda. Under these headings came the referendums or plebiscites extensively practised under Louis-Napoleon Bonaparte, and improvised by the adventurer Georges Boulanger in 1887-8.[20] It remains possible and not unreasonable for readers of Paragraph 5 to identify such recourse to the popular will rather than a general election along British lines. And here again, the Proclamation (its intentions never implemented by its sponsors) differs from the electoral circumstances leading to the establishment of Dáil Éireann.

De Paor held that its basic features were decided by late January 1916, after the IRB's three-day enforced discussion with James Connolly. With drafts by Pearse and Connolly, reviewed by MacDonagh, the text evolved informally and secretly. No legal expertise appears to have been consulted. Delays in New York or Germany rendered the final timing rushed, all the more so when the Plunkett-forged Castle Document and the broader deception of MacNeill by his subordinates added to confusion.[21] Nevertheless, the Proclamation was successfully printed, ready for Easter weekend.

In the second part of *On the Easter Proclamation*, de Paor generally allocates several pages per paragraph. For Paragraph 5 he provides fewer than 150 words, plus a quotation (almost as long) from Ruth Dudley Edwards's biography of Pearse. It is on the whole acceptable to historian and analyst alike, though his verdict rests largely on the issue of female suffrage. There is, however, one strikingly negative comment. While he finds the statement of intent 'truthful and sincere' he promptly qualifies this—'in the strange circumstances it is the statement of a junta executing a coup'.[22] The mix of

**20** See Ian Bullock and Siân Reynolds, 'Direct Legislation and Socialism: How British and French Socialists Viewed the Referendum in the 1890s', *History Workshop*, no. 24 (1987), pp 62–81. **21** For some useful detail, see Tom Reilly, *Joe Stanley, Printer to the Rising* (Dingle: Brandon, 2005), p. 120 etc. **22** De Paor, *On the Easter Proclamation*, p. 77. This was not de Paor's only note of extreme caution in characterising the signatories' approval, sharp disengagement and reliance on an unconfirmed source should persuade us to think deeply about Paragraph 5 and de Paor's commentary. At its core lies the fundamental issue of sovereignty.

Sovereignty would take us well beyond the confines of an introduction. So let us turn to Dudley Edwards as quoted. She had been in acidulous mood:

> The revolutionaries had made some small provision for the day of victory, however unlikely. A provisional government, less abhorrent to the people than they were, had been selected—Alderman Tom Kelly, Arthur Griffith, William O'Brien, Mrs Sheehy-Skeffington and Seán T. O'Kelly (Sinn Féin, Sinn Féin, Labour, Suffragette-socialist and Sinn Féin respectively). It is most unlikely that any of these prominent citizens knew of the august role for which they had been chosen—except O'Kelly, who was secretly a member of the IRB, and was to suffer some anguish after his arrest lest the British authorities should have discovered his 'importance'; in case Tom Kelly refused the chair, Seán T. was to direct the civil government.[23]

De Paor knew the author of this well; he was a colleague of her father Robin Dudley Edwards, professor of Irish History at UCD. As he accepted her reliability on a substantial claim, we might be inclined to pass over it also. However, Dr Dudley Edwards left her information untraceable through footnotes. She listed three general sources for the sub-chapter in question, written by Desmond FitzGerald, Diarmuid Lynch and Desmond Ryan, all veterans of the GPO. We can certify that neither *Desmond's Rising: Memoirs 1913 to Easter 1916* nor Lynch's writings as edited by Florence O'Donoghue hint at any second-row civilian Provisional or National Government. Ryan's *The Rising: the Complete Story of Easter Week* (which Dudley Edwards specified) is equally unsupportive of her.[24]

---

underlying position. About the opening paragraph – 'In the name of God and of the dead generations ...' – he remarked that 'the words are a call to a jihad' (p. 46).   **23** Ruth Dudley Edwards, *Patrick Pearse: the Triumph of Failure* (London: Gollancz, 1977), p. 276. **24** Dudley Edwards's unacknowledged source was the memoir, *Forth the Banners Go* (1969) by William O'Brien. From this it is clear that Connolly had been to the fore in advising O'Brien of his possible future role in a civilian provisional government 'whose duties would include looking after food supplies and transport'. O'Brien had earlier published an

Whatever about its veracity, the list of nominees raises a question central to any apprehension of democratic freedom. Either the five were chosen by the clandestine seven-man Military Council, or simply by Pearse and Connolly in tandem. Thus approved, few others could hope to win out in the armed 'elections' for the *permanent* (please note) National Government. Who else would have the right or power to nominate additional names? Was this not a slate—perhaps including some of the victorious signatories—to be presented in a plebiscite allowing only a yes or no response, in effect a nominated assembly along Cromwellian lines? Of course, the seven were not victorious, and no slate was put to 'the whole people' except in the 1918 UK general election, by which time some women had been enfranchised. At this point, it is perhaps enough to say that the words 'democratic' or 'democracy' feature nowhere in the Proclamation.[25]

Around the fringes of the Second International and outside, radically new ideas of revolution were growing. Syndicalism, in its separate American and French developments, focused on industry as the defining role of the worker, subsuming older notions of citizenship, free-holding, property-ownership and so forth. As early as 1905, soviets (or workers' councils) were organised in parts of the Russian empire. Much of the theoretical basis of *industrie* was French, with Sorel adding a distinctive element of constructive violence. Fear of syndicalism spread in Britain, a factor which may partly explain repeated press claims that alien influences were at work in Dublin in 1913 and again in 1916.[26]

Connolly was well aware of these new forces, mainly through his American work. *The Workers' Republic* of 22 September 1900 carried a very cogent *exposé* of 'parliamentary democracy', its inherent class bias and its structural provisions to ensure that end. His article concluded:

account in the introduction to *Labour and Easter Week*, ed. Desmond Ryan (Dublin: Three Candles Press, 1949). **25** The ease with which these terms were conveniently assumed to be present is indicated in Joost Augusteijn, *Patrick Pearse: the Making of a Revolutionary* (Basingstoke: Palgrave, 2010). The Proclamation 'tried to encompass all the Irish including Protestants and the poor by the promise to cherish "all the children of the nation equally" and institute a fully representative democratic government' (p. 309). **26** For a well-informed, if generally unsympathetic, account of Sorel, see Isaiah Berlin, *Against the Grain: Essays in the History of Ideas* (London: Pimlico, 1997), pp 296–332. The essay carefully distinguishes between Sorel's positions and those of active French syndicalists, while perhaps exaggerating his influence on the student protest movements of the 1960s and '70s.

The freedom of the revolutionist will change the choice of rulers which we have today into the choice of administrators of laws voted upon directly by the people; and will also substitute for the choice of masters (capitalists) the appointment of reliable public servants under direct public control. That will mean true democracy—the industrial democracy of the Socialist Republic.[27]

'Industrial democracy' had been put into circulation by Sidney and Beatrice Webb with their two-volume *Industrial Democracy* (1897), a distinctly Fabian work concerned with the internal organisation of trade unions and the legal position of unions vis-a-vis employers and government. The Industrial Workers of the World (founded 1905) and syndicalists in France advocated versions of industrial democracy, the latter being the more thoroughly radical. If it is conceded that both this passage of 1900 and Paragraph 5 of 1916 allude to direct democracy, then the influence of Connolly on the paragraph's composition is virtually established. Within a wider timeframe, one should locate Connolly's traceable promotion of industrial democracy—essentially, political participation through trade-union membership—earlier than 1916. The article just quoted appeared in September 1900; in the same month, the Irish Socialist Republican Party sent three delegates to the Second International's Paris Congress, a high point of Irish interest in European socialism. It is unlikely that Connolly was one of the three.[28]

The impact of continental ideas on Irish radicalism in the early part of the twentieth century deserves more consideration than it has received to date. One strand of influence relates to French right-wing nationalism not only in its political forms but also its cultural manifestations in literature, philosophy and Catholic thinking.[29] Another spins out from the gradual breakdown of the Second International, the challenges to 'orthodox' socialism from various quarters, most forcefully through Sorel's writings. That is for another occasion. To conclude however, by attempting to see

---

**27** James Connolly, *Lost writings*, ed. Aindreas O Cathasaigh (London: Pluto, 2007), p. 48. See Richard Vernon, '"Citizenship" in "Industry"; the case of George Sorel', *The American Political Science Review*, vol. 75, no. 1 (March 1981), pp 17–28. **28** For the background, and the reasons for concluding that the delegation did not include Connolly, see David Lynch, *Radical Politics in Modern Ireland: the Irish Socialist Republican Party 1896–1904* (Dublin: Irish Academic Press, 2005), passim, esp. pp 102–3, n30. **29** See W.J. Mc Cormack, *Dublin 1916: the French Connection* (Dublin: Gill and Macmillan, 2012).

the Easter Proclamation not just through its second to last paragraph but as a whole, not just in its local historical context but in a contemporary European one also, let me end with a relatively recent summary of Henry Bergson's philosophy of *durée*:

> Pure duration is what is most removed from externality and least penetrated with externality, a duration in which the past is big with a present absolutely new. But then our will is strained to the utmost; we have to gather up the past which is slipping away, and thrust it whole and undivided into the present. At such moments we truly possess ourselves, but such moments are rare. Duration is the very stuff of reality, which is perpetual becoming, never something made.[30]

As an abstract summary of the Sinn Féin IRB outlook embodied in the Proclamation, this could hardly be bettered. Its author was Bertrand Russell. It may be dismissed as an irrelevance in the seminar of hard knocks which is the Irish historical profession. De Paor's book about the document is the most thorough I have encountered, unique in its combining exposition and critique.

## V: A NOTE ON THE TEXT

For the sake of clarity, the book of 1997 has been for this new edition renamed *The Easter Proclamation (1916): a Comparative Analysis*. Inconsistencies of initial capitalisation have been standardised, and a very small number of typos silently corrected. I have expanded some of the endnotes, providing more details of de Paor's sources. The text itself is reproduced verbatim.

---

**30** Bertrand Russell, *A History of Western Philosophy* (2nd ed., London: Allen & Unwin, 1961), pp 759–60.

# Preface by the author

This is an essay on words. It is concerned primarily, not with the events leading up to the 1916 Rising in Ireland, still less with the Rising itself or its aftermath, but with the text of the declaration announcing that action, and with the ideas and echoes to be found in the text.

Outside the General Post Office in Dublin on Easter Monday, 1916, at the beginning of the armed insurrection which then took place against the British government of Ireland, P.H. Pearse read aloud the Proclamation of an Irish Republic. The text he read contains 486 words, not counting the subscriptions of names. It is the apologia of the uprising, a statement of purpose and intent.

'All changed, changed utterly', Yeats wrote about the effects of the Easter Rising. The Rising deflected the course of Irish history. The present Irish state owes, if not its being, at least its shape to it. The Proclamation therefore has some considerable historical interest. It is of present-day interest too, for citizens of the Republic of Ireland. It declares the Republic's raison d'être and announces, very briefly, what kind of state was intended. It expounds some ideas clearly enough and a few less clearly. It was restated and ratified by the elected deputies assembled for the first Dáil Éireann in January 1919 and thereby given the force of a mandate of a majority of the people of Ireland, and, although it was superseded by the Articles of Agreement of 1921, as ratified by the Dáil in 1922, and by the Constitution of the Irish Free State, its principles were embodied, in some part, in the new Constitution enacted by the electorate of the Irish Free State in 1937, and its memory, if nothing more, was revived when the government in Dublin declared the Irish state to be a republic and this received international acknowledgment, including British recognition in 1949.[1]

The words of the Proclamation were put together by P.H. Pearse and revised by James Connolly and Thomas MacDonagh, the main draft coming, it would seem, from the pen of Pearse, but with certain important additions from the thought of Connolly: in the period immediately before the Rising each man had much influenced the other in his view of what they were about. The document is short and exhortatory, offering comparatively small purchase for exegesis. Nonetheless, teased out, it unfolds patterns of thought and, perhaps more revealingly, assumptions worth examining. It is an essay in a genre.

The genre is exemplified in the American Declaration of Independence, of 1776, which for that reason will be discussed briefly here; but the Irish Proclamation is quite unlike the American Declaration in important respects and does not emerge from a similar complexity of political and philosophical debate; it issues not only from wholly different circumstances but from a different view of the world. Yet it shows a remote influence of the American document, and, like it, attempts a formal announcement of high purpose.

There can be little doubt that, had the Rising never happened, an autonomous Irish state would still have come into being. A Home Rule Act, sought by Irish nationalist parliamentarians for more than three decades but most bitterly opposed by Irish unionists (notably in Ulster), was already on the British statute book, although not only had its operation been suspended until the end of the Great War then being waged, but there was a probability of drastic amendment to exclude Ulster or part of it. As enacted by the parliament of the United Kingdom in 1914, it purported to confer limited legislative and severely limited executive independence on the people of the island as a whole. But, in view of the continuing and vehement opposition to it, we can have no idea what course the history of such independence would have followed; although we may guess that, had the path of Home Rule been pursued until tens of thousands of Irish soldiers returned from the Great War, there might well have ensued a bitter civil war between Orange and Green. But we have for our scrutiny only the Irish state which actually exists, not one which might have been.

# On the Easter Proclamation
# and Other Declarations

The Republic of Ireland came into being through a fuzzy mixture of accident and design. This is usual in history; in the course of events 'as they actually happened'. But those who maintain the public institutions seize on the moments when design seems supreme. Modern states like to think that they exist by intent and purpose; that God, or patriarchal founders, or ancestral wisdom, or perhaps just the spirit of the race, predestined their present order or some ideal version of it. Such intentions are cast in bronze and graven in stone. For the Irish state the solemn statement of purpose, *aere perennius*, is the Proclamation of the Irish Republic at Easter 1916.

Yet, even the moments of most obvious design acquire a character of serendipitous inconsequence when we examine them closely. Contingency and accident dog the noble purpose. Such solemn pronouncements of intent as the American Declaration of Independence or the French Declaration of the Rights of Man and of the Citizen—or the Communist Manifesto of 1848, portentous as it is—turn out to be, at least in part, hasty improvisations to give direction and meaning to something that is already happening, rather than long-considered blueprints for a happy and glorious future.

The Founding Fathers of the American Republic did not initially gather in long conclave in order to plan the details of a radically new political society (although something like this happened in the summer of 1787, when they had to face the consequences of what they had brought about; when they drafted the Constitution). On the contrary, the representatives of the thirteen colonies, assembled in congress in Philadelphia to petition the king, came very slowly, and some of them most reluctantly, to the conclusion in 1776 that, since they had been at war with the 'mother country' for a year or so, and there was no self-respecting way for them to back out of it, the time had come to cut the apron strings. So they deputed one of their number, Thomas Jefferson, who had the gift of words and had taken leisure to give previous thought and attention to such matters, to draft a lofty justification.

The Declaration he wrote has five parts: 1: a protestation that the people of the colonies have been forced to the action they are taking; it is not their fault; 2: an affirmation of 'self-evident' truths concerning political society and the relationship of governors to the governed; 3: a long recital of grievances; 4: the statement that the connection with England is *now* severed and that the thirteen colonies are, *as of now*, free, sovereign and independent states (a declaration of an existential change, the declaration itself constituting a rite of passage); 5: a solemn covenant (distinctly Protestant in its concept) of mutual commitment of life, property and honour, under God, for the support of the declared independence.

In its opening, the document protests that the colonies had been driven to sever the ties only when the mother country met their loyalty with cold injustice:

> When in the course of human events, it becomes necessary for one people to dissolve the political bonds which have connected them with another, and to assume among the powers of the earth, the separate and equal station to which the Laws of Nature and of Nature's God entitle them, a decent respect to the opinions of mankind requires that they should declare the causes which impel them to the Separation.[2]

The statement is argumentative from the start, and somewhat defensively so. Jefferson's first draft had contained the sentence, even more passively phrased: 'We acquiesce in the necessity which pronounces our everlasting Adieu.' The main body of the document 'declares the causes which impel them to the Separation': a lengthy recital of the grievances that had driven the colonials to an extreme. These, on the whole, repeat the grievances of previous petitions to the crown, but the members of the congress now restate them as reproaches. The colonial worthies were, with trepidation, finally breaking with mother country and father king, and now it is upon the royal head that they heap blame after blame for the perverse denial of paternal love. But should not even the unnatural parent be obeyed? Is this not God's law? To answer such questions, which had caused some anguish in colonial bosoms in the previous ten years, the members of the congress preceded the recital of grievances with a short and somewhat glib summary of the principles that animated their political being. They did not intend a statement of something new, but a restatement of propositions

they took to be historic and ancient (as if in the spirit of Protestant reformation returning to biblical roots). In the years gone by, some of them
had been troubled in their souls by the dilemma: how could they reconcile with their traditional and sentimental attachment to the British connection the outrage they felt at British arrogance (as they saw it) in
dismissing their complaints? They represented assemblies which had for
the most part been self-ruling—subject to minor limitations—for generations, and they possessed charters of liberties deriving from a long history
of ordered and acknowledged government. They had searched arduously
for the wellsprings of their political society and had come to attempt a formulation of universal principles. 'We hold these truths to be self-evident.'
Self-evidence, a category established in Enlightenment thought, is the
most expedient kind of evidence for question-begging, since it precludes
the need for arguing a case; and the case the colonials were making was a
rationalization:

> That all men are created equal, that they are endowed by their
> Creator with certain unalienable Rights, that among these are Life,
> Liberty and the pursuit of Happiness.—That to secure these rights
> Governments are instituted among men, deriving their just power
> from the consent of the governed.

This was a fashionable, but controversial rather than self-evident, theory,
which had come to be widely accepted. It had offered up to this point a
harmless (because purely theoretical) explanation of the original nature of
political society. Now it was to be given a positive practical force. The
unoriginality of the Declaration has often been noted, not least by
Jefferson's colleagues and contemporaries, who sometimes accused him of
plagiarism or triteness or both. His draft was subject to only a little emen-
dation by the Continental Congress—an indication that such ideas as it
contained had become commonplace. His achievement was to make
sonorous and succinct the enunciation of a philosophy, current at the
time, that well suited the present purpose. His Declaration implicitly
invokes the 'natural law' of compact.

In embryo, or rather in infancy, the theory of the 'social contract' may
be found in some medieval analyses of political society; notably in the
Aristotelianism of St Thomas ('*Civitas est nonnisi congregatio hominum ...*':
'the State is nothing but the congregation of people ...'). The theory had

further developed partly through long and confused quarrels, significantly for the present purpose in seventeenth-century England, Scotland and Ireland, between the pretensions of absolute monarchs and the resistance of intransigent subjects, giving rise to researches into the sources of ancient liberties and to discussions of the origins of authority in government. To a partial reading of Magna Carta and similar historic definitions of liberties were added the teachings of Hobbes and others, including Hutcheson, Hume, Rousseau and Locke (more, it would now seem, in his *Essay Concerning the Human Understanding* than in his *Second Treatise on Government*). The primal, or 'natural', freedom on which the social contract was founded was thought to be acknowledged in the English Constitution deriving from the 'Glorious Revolution' of 1688–9 ('revolution' in this sense meaning an orderly rotation of government such as occurs in modern states after general elections). This, it was held, had restored traditional liberties safeguarded by the contract between king and subjects. The 'liberties of Englishmen' were commonly stated as the objective of the colonials in their struggle with king and parliament.

In the theoretical part of the Declaration Jefferson drew on 'the harmonizing sentiments of the day', as he put it himself, and echoed the Scot, James Wilson, who had recently written that:

> All men are, by nature, equal and free: no one has a right to any authority over another without his consent: all lawful government is founded on the consent of those who are subject to it: such consent was given with a view to ensure and to increase the happiness of the governed, above what they could enjoy in an independent and unconnected state of nature. The consequence is, that the happiness of the society is the *first* law of every government;[3]

and the Virginia Declaration of Rights (June, 1776), drafted by George Mason, which declared:

> That all men are by nature equally free and independent, and have certain inherent rights, of which, when they enter into a state of society, they cannot by any compact deprive or divest their posterity; namely, the enjoyment of life and liberty, with the means of acquiring and possessing property, and pursuing and obtaining happiness and safety ...[4]

The recital of the grievances which gave rise to the act of separation is directed personally to the king, George III; but at its conclusion those issuing the Declaration turn to the king's subjects in the home country and say that they have warned their 'British brethren' from time to time of what was happening:

> They too have been deaf to the voice of justice and of consanguinity. We must, therefore, acquiesce in the necessity, which denounces our Separation, and hold them, as we hold the rest of mankind, Enemies in War, in Peace Friends.

This in effect renounces the special relationship of 'consanguinity' which had connected the American colonials to the people of the home countries (although the makeup of the colonial population at the time was such that the claimed consanguinity was less than the protesters suggested) and places George III's subjects at home on the same plane as the rest of the human race so far as the Americans are, from now on, concerned. The blood of the connection, or its image in American minds, was in due course to prove thicker than water, giving rise after a century to a later 'special relationship', but the formal position, once the Declaration took effect, was that the British were no more than another foreign people.

The final paragraph sets forth formally the act of separation, which is immediately followed by the covenant of the new states' representatives (a covenant deriving from the pledge of mutual support which had bound together the first congress): the germ of the Constitution of the new republic:

> We, therefore, the Representatives of the united States of America, in General Congress, Assembled, appealing to the Supreme Judge of the world for the rectitude of our intention, do, in the Name, and by the Authority of the good people of these Colonies, solemnly publish and declare, That these United Colonies are, and of Right ought to be Free and Independent States; that they are Absolved from all Allegiance to the British Crown, and that all political connection between them and the State of Great Britain, is and ought to be totally dissolved; and that as Free and Independent States, they have full power to levy War, conclude Peace, contract Alliances, establish Commerce, and do all other

Acts and Things which Independent States may of right do.—And for the support of this Declaration, with a firm reliance on the Protection of Divine Providence, we mutually pledge to each other our Lives, our Fortunes and our sacred Honor.

After some emendations and excisions, the Declaration was approved by the congress on 4 July and was hastily printed in Philadelphia that night by John Dunlap for distribution throughout the colonies (now states) and beyond. Its punctuation and capitalization were criticized; it was a rushed and botched job (at least in its presentation). And its principal author, Jefferson, regarded the changes made by the congress as 'mutilation' of his art.

But it worked the magic. The United States of America is a great country founded on an idea. Yet this is not what the Founding Fathers, initially, set out to do. When Jefferson, following half a dozen precedents, put forward the 'truth' that 'all men are created equal', he was not quite making the political philosophical statement which that instantly became; but was rather repeating a truism about 'Nature and Nature's God', about human nature, and about the human condition in the 'state of nature' *before* people entered into the social contract: we all start fom the same scratch line, helpless, weak and puling. But he went on to say that, precedent to political society, God had endowed us, already in that state of nature, with certain 'unalienable rights'. From its context, this assertion about the rights of those hypothetical people who existed before political society came into being, enjoying all the liberties of what might be described as an amoebal freedom, became applicable to people *within* political society. God has not appointed our rulers; he has given us 'unalienable rights'. In the perceived theory of the new dispensation, 'rights' superseded both laws and the prescription of custom. And they included the dangerous right (whose implication in the contract was accepted) to rebel:

That whenever any form of Government becomes destructive of these ends, it is the Right of the People to alter or abolish it, and to institute new Powers from the consent of the governed.

Contrast with this an older teaching, as in the words of Martin Luther, written in Wittenberg in 1521:

> ... hence no insurrection is just, no matter how just the cause it stands for. I support, and will always support the party who suffers the insurrection, no matter how unjust their cause, and will always oppose the party who make insurrection, no matter how just their cause, for the reason that insurrection can never happen without the shedding of innocent blood.[5]

The Founding Fathers, however, did not intend to be radical, although there were radicals among them. But they were forced by the circumstances of a conflict, in which they had the choice to yield and perish or to go all out and win, to an act of separation so radical in itself that they were at a loss to find a sufficiently conservative justification for it. They tried; but their justification immediately became the charter of a new political age.

So much did it become this that we can't even begin to consider the sources of the Proclamation of the Irish Republic issued in Dublin on Easter Monday 1916 without turning first to the American Declaration of Independence. That Declaration from the moment of its promulgation became a model and an exemplar, and its phrases and affirmations were to be echoed in declarations, manifestos and proclamations around the world.

There is a very special link with the Irish Proclamation. The news of the American rebellion brought both joy and immediate emulation in Ireland, initially in colonial Ireland, and set in train a history of which the Easter Proclamation was one among innumerable consequences. Both the American statement and the Irish one of 140 years later renounced the same crown. One signalled the breakup of the first British empire. The other signalled the breakup of the second British empire. And for 140 years before 1916, America had been for Irish patriots and nationalists the Promised Land; not just a haven for emigrants, but the home of the free and—in time—an example for democrats. However, it must also be said that the two documents are remarkably unlike. They proceed from different premises and much of the feeling of the American document would be expressed better in the tenets of Irish unionism than in the affirmations of Irish nationalism.

Before comparing them, it is necessary to look at the other document which, in important ways, was a resource for the Easter Proclamation: the French Declaration of the Rights of Man and of the Citizen, of August 1789.[6] This in turn, of course, was heavily influenced by the American

Declaration, from which it is separated in time by only thirteen years; yet it has a different significance. The American Declaration emanates from the deliberations of the representatives of thirteen disparate colonies, brought together in the second 'Continental Congress' by common interests and common grievances in the face of British government (which they saw as misgovernment) but fully answerable to the separate colonial bodies that had sent them to Philadelphia. They were no more than feeling their way towards a common American 'nationality', which was to be arbitrarily defined, excluding, for example, Canada. Their Declaration opens with a somewhat ambiguous expression: 'When it becomes necessary for *one people* to dissolve the political bonds which have connected them with *another* ...' This is either a general or a particular statement. It sets forth a principle applicable to any 'people'. It leaves open the question whether 'one people' is a general and exemplary term, to refer to 'the people of Virginia', 'the people of Pennsylvania', and so on, or whether Jefferson was in these words being particular and speaking for 'one people', the White colonial people, or the male White colonial English-speaking propertied people, of America. The core of the Declaration is unambiguously plural in this respect: 'We ... the representatives of the united States of America, in General Congress, Assembled ...' The erratic capitalization of the document is revealing, for a little further on, the word 'united' is given a capital: '... these United Colonies are, and of Right ought to be Free and Independent States ...' A union of a kind—of interest, of purpose, and of military endeavour—already existed among the colonies to justify the capital letter in 'United' here; the question whether the newly independent states would remain in union, or how, was for the moment open, and the new states are 'united', not 'United'. A nation had been conceived but was not yet born, and the Declaration did not purport to be the outline of a constitution for a new country, although the germ of such a constitution lay in the covenant embodied in its final sentence. (It should be noted that the name of the new country, 'the United States of America', was plural in general usage until the Civil War of 1861–5— 'The United States of America *are* ...'—but became singular after that war—'The United States of America *is* ...')

The Declaration is not necessarily a republican document. It names God as the source of the rights it asserts. Governments instituted to protect these rights derive 'their just powers from the consent of the governed'. The members of the congress would have admitted that such rights were enjoyed by Englishmen, under their king. The French Declaration names a different source for 'the Rights of Man and of the Citizen'—nature. All men are born with equal rights, which are, 'of nature', inalienable and sacred. The National Assembly, however, 'recognizes and declares, in the presence of the Supreme Being, and with the hope of his blessing and favour, the following sacred rights of men and of citizens ...' This is the only reference to divinity; but the first printing of the French Declaration for distribution was headed by the Masonic symbol of the all-seeing eye of God within a triangle, such as may be seen at the apex of a pyramid on the back of a US dollar bill (all but a handful of the signatories of the American Declaration were Freemasons). The symbol is described at the foot of the page bearing the French Declaration as 'The supreme eye of reason, which has just dissipated the obscuring clouds.' The American Declaration is hesitantly deist; the French is whole-heartedly secular. Or, as Karl Barth put it:

> The Calvinism gone to seed of the American document still distinguished itself from the Catholicism gone to seed of the French one.[7]

And the French Declaration was, by intent, constitutional. It was issued on 26 August 1789, by a meeting, the first to be summoned for 175 years, of the Estates General of France, a convocation which, in the course of confusion so great that to the present day nobody can explain satisfactorily exactly what was happening, had reconstituted itself as a National Constituent Assembly, dedicated to the writing of a constitution for France. The Declaration was intended as a statement of principle to form the basis for this new constitution. It, and the constitution duly founded on it and adopted on 3 September 1791, set out to create a limited or constitutional monarchy, broadly copied from that of Great Britain. The supreme authority in the state was no longer to be the king, in his divine right, but the nation, whose general will was expressed through this assembly and its successors. In the deliberations of the time (not only in France) it is both implicit and explicit that the general will of the nation was not to be ascertained by the balancing of interests through adversarial disputes of factions or parties—which were thought of as hostile or detrimental to the public good—but was to emerge through the medium of the people's representatives by a kind of ventriloquism.

The Declaration of the Rights of Man and of the Citizen states that men are born free and equal, and remain so in their rights to liberty, property and safety and the right to resist oppression. 'The Nation is essentially the source of all sovereignty', and is the source of authority. Government exists to maintain the citizen's rights. The only limit to the liberty of one is the liberty and rights of others. Laws (which may prohibit only what is harmful to society) shall determine these limits to liberty; but no one may be held guilty except by due process of law. The citizen has full freedom of expression, short of endangering the public peace, as defined by law. Property is inviolable, except where public necessity, as laid down by law, requires otherwise; and then full compensation must be paid. Those enforcing the law do so in the public interest, not their own. Every citizen is entitled to take part in the formulation of law, which is the expression of the general will. Taxation must be equitably distributed and imposed only by the consent of the citizens, who are entitled to resist whenever their rights are not guaranteed.

In this formulation, and in the constitution which ensued, the sovereign nation, a new legal entity, became supreme. The king became 'King of the French', no longer 'King of France'. Citizenship and nationality were defined. As Louis XVI put it early in 1790:

> The sovereign nation now has only citizens equal in rights, no other despot but the law, no agents but public servants; and the King is the first of them. Such is the French Revolution.[8]

This declaration, like the Declaration of Independence, did not proclaim a republic; nor is a republican constitution necessarily implied in the intentions of the framers of either. Yet in both, the source of authority is stated to be, not the king under God, but 'the consent of the governed' (i.e., of 'the people') or the 'general will'. Both declare certain human rights to be antecedent to and independent of law and external authority. Both led, within a short space of time, to the setting up of republican states. The Americans decided to strengthen their union and form a single nation (although the singularity was to remain ambiguous for a considerable time, until it was redefined in a few phrases by Lincoln in 1863). Jefferson, the principal author of the Declaration, chose for the nation newly formed from the thirteen colonies the motto of a popular periodical of the time, the *Gentleman's Magazine*, which brought between a single pair of covers a great miscellany of news and musings (a 'magazine', on the analogy of a general store of goods) and summed up its achievement in the words *'E pluribus unum'*. The French, having abolished the ancient provinces with their disparate characters in favour of the departments of a nation with a single general will, soon abandoned the constitution of 1791, and emulated the English of 1649 (who had declared that 'the people are, under God, the original of all just power' and had proceeded to proclaim the supremacy of 'the Commons of England, in Parliament assembled, being chosen by and representing the people'.) The French killed the king whose semi-divine fatherhood they had renounced, just as the English had done in 1649.

In Ireland, the leaders of the colony, and of the political nation, first demanded the rights of Americans (who had demanded the rights of Englishmen) while aiding the British war effort by raising an army of volunteers to replace the troops sent to suppress the American rebellion and to oppose the French allies of the rebels. When they had that volunteer army at their back, they too, or a sufficient number among them, attempted a declaration of independence. Grattan moved it in the House of Commons in Dublin on 19 April 1780:

> What! Has England lost thirteen provinces? Has she reconciled herself to this loss, and will she not be reconciled to the liberty of Ireland? Take notice that the very Constitution which I move you to declare, Great Britain herself offered to America; it is a very instructive proceeding in British history. In 1778 a commission went out, with powers to cede to the thirteen provinces of America, totally and radically, the legislative authority claimed over her by the British Parliament, and the Commissioners, pursuant to their powers, did offer to all, or any, of the American States, the total surrender of the legislative authority of the British Parliament. I will read their letter to the Congress ... What! Has England offered this to the resistance of America, and will she refuse it to the loyalty of Ireland?
>
> I will not be answered by a public lie, in the shape of an amendment; neither, speaking for the subjects' freedom, am I to hear of faction. I wish for nothing but to breathe, in this our island, in common with my fellow subjects, the air of liberty. I have no ambition, unless it be the ambition to break your chain, and

contemplate your glory. I never will be satisfied so long as the meanest cottager in Ireland has a link to the British chain clanking to his rags; he may be naked, he shall not be in irons; and I do see the time is at hand, the spirit is gone forth, the declaration is planted; and though great men should apostatize, yet the cause will lie; and though the public speaker should die, yet the immortal fire shall outlast the organ which conveyed it, and the breath of liberty, like the word of the holy man, will not die with the prophet, but survive him.

I shall move you, 'That the King's most excellent Majesty, and the Lords and Commons of Ireland, are the only power competent to make laws to bind Ireland.'[9]

This declaration was in line with what the Americans had been demanding before 1776: the right, under the crown, to legislate for and tax themselves, and to petition the crown directly, freed from the rule of the British parliament. It is a demand that was to be renewed on Ireland's behalf from time to time for more than a century; but at that time it was essentially the demand of the colonial public, which held eighteenth-century Ireland for the crown and for the British empire in and beyond Ireland. The members of that public were tipsy with a new self-assurance. 'Never was there a Parliament in Ireland so possessed of the confidence of the people', as Grattan put it:

—you are the greatest political assembly now sitting in the world; not only do we possess an unconquerable force, but a certain unquenchable fire, which has touched all ranks of men like a visitation.

They sought freedom to come to terms independently with the mass of the Irish people and to form a union within Ireland (where the most numerous class of people, the Catholics, had been excluded by law from participation in political and professional life, but must, somehow, be reckoned with). And they had their moment; but it passed with the end of the century. England's loss of America in the war which was being concluded as he spoke, moved Grattan to say, in the course of the same speech:

> There is no policy left for Great Britain but to cherish the remains of her empire, and do justice to a country who is determined to do justice to herself, certain that she gives nothing equal to what she received from us when we gave her Ireland.

But it was not to be.

The rhetoric of the American Revolution is echoed already in Grattan's words of 1780; the rhetoric of the French Revolution was soon to echo in Ireland too. For that colonial public which had 'given' Ireland to Great Britain failed, with legislative independence (obtained in 1782), to achieve any real independence of action, and in particular to sustain the military independence from which its power had derived; and it failed, secondly, to make a union within Ireland. The French example was irresistible to Irish sans-culottes and colonial romantics, and its slogans were to echo, sometimes muffled, sometimes distorted, through speeches, programmes, manifestos and proclamations, down to the extraordinary decade in Ireland that began with the introduction in Westminster of the Third Home Rule Bill in 1912.

By then the basic political principles which the authors of the American and French declarations had found it necessary to spell out were absorbed into the commonplace of political thought, and in the process overlaid by other, sometimes contrary, ideas. The document of 1916 is an instrument of hostile separation, but it is fundamentally different from the American Declaration in that it is oblivious of the union it proposes to end; it proclaims not so much separation as a mystically pre-existing independence: there never has been a union (except in mere fact); in true reality, Ireland always has been, and now *declares herself to be*, independent. And it is to be noted that this declaration does not purport to be made by any body of representatives in congress or otherwise assembled, but by the personified nation.

Secondarily, but importantly, the Proclamation is a sketchy outline of the constitution of an independent Irish state. It is not, like the American Declaration, a justification for an action reluctantly taken. It ignores, arrogantly, all the existing constitutional arrangements, granting them no legitimacy. It purports to be (although it does not explicitly say so) an affirmation of the general will, a general will ascertained not by the processes of the available political arrangements, which were deemed to have failed and to be irrelevant to the present purpose, but by the intuition of the group of philosopher kings who issued it, who, as Socrates said (according to Plato):

> will take as their canvas a State and the characters of people; and they will, first, make their canvas clean—no easy matter. But that is just the point, in which they will differ from all others. They will refuse to take in hand either individual or State (nor will they draft laws) before they either received a clean canvas or have made it clean themselves.[10]

The Easter Proclamation is more than an echo. It is, in its turn, the founders' announcement of a new state. How was it put together and what does it say?

The Supreme Council of the Irish Republican Brotherhood, a secret society, had initially deputed three men to plan the rising, in close consultation with two members of the Council who had most firmly resolved to bring it about. These had brought in two more, and in the end it was on their own initiative they issued the Proclamation, which all seven signed. The Easter Rising was organized by a conspiracy in which there were secrets within secrets, most of them successfully kept. Because of this success, the conspiracy is only sketchily documented, and much remains, and will remain, unknown.

The idea of a rising had been cherished by separatist groups down the years since before the Union which came into effect on 1 January 1801. Attempts to put the idea into practice, by Robert Emmet and other survivors of the United Irishmen in 1803, by members of Young Ireland in 1848, and by the Fenians in 1867, failed miserably, although Emmet's conspiracy was detailed and fully thought out and the Fenian organization was extensive and numerous. But in spite of failure (political as well as military) the Fenian tradition was maintained, and by the early twentieth century the intention of rising against British rule was promoted principally in two closely connected secret societies, both of which conducted open as well as hidden activities. These were Clan na Gael in the United States and the Irish Revolutionary (later 'Republican') Brotherhood in Ireland. Towards the end of the nineteenth century the IRB had greatly diminished both in numbers and in revolutionary fervour, but it was stimulated into renewed vigour after the temporary collapse of nationalist parliamentary politics that ensued on the fall of Parnell and his death in 1891.

That fall induced in nationalist Ireland a decade-long depression of spirit and a widespread revulsion against the apparently pointless activities and plainly shabby quarrelling of what had been Parnell's disciplined party, now split. And, as Tom Garvin has pointed out,[11] Ireland shared in the general effects of modernization and social and political change at the end of the century, including the rise of movements of 'extremely romantic and visionary character'. Nationalism of various shades and denominations continued to flourish, but many people chose to express it in ways other than the politics of Parnell's successors, John Redmond, Tim Healy, John Dillon and T.P. O'Connor—through the attempts to preserve and revive the Irish language, sponsored chiefly by the Gaelic League (founded in 1893); through the revival of 'Gaelic' games under the auspices of the Gaelic Athletic Association (founded in 1884); through the creation of a new Irish literature and drama; through alternative forms of politics, as in the self-sufficiency programme embodied in Edward Martyn's and Arthur Griffith's 'Sinn Féin' organization (founded in 1905).

The Fenian tradition offered another alternative. Fenianism, which had wholly failed in its efforts to organize a nationwide rising against British rule in the 1860s, was radically separatist; but organized Fenianism had been prepared to back the 'Land War' and to give Parnell his chance to win limited self-government for Ireland. Parnell in turn found in Fenianism the necessary background menace to make persuasive his parliamentary arguments, and he offered to the Fenians the hope that self-government under Home Rule would not forever be limited:

> We cannot, under the British Constitution, ask for more than the restitution of Grattan's Parliament, but no man has a right to fix the boundary of the march of a nation. No man has a right to say 'Thus far shalt thou go and no further'; and we have never attempted to fix the *ne plus ultra* to the progress of Ireland's nationhood, and we never shall.[12]

After his fall, that stratagem was abandoned, although John Redmond, who had remained loyal to Parnell, initially acknowledged that the potential of some form of force was necessary to back argument in dealing with the British government. But he moved on to accept (as did many of his contemporaries throughout the world) that future world power lay with the British empire, remodelled as a global federation of self-governing

English-speaking peoples, and with a few other dominant nations (including the USA, which, in 1898, had taken up 'the White Man's burden'), and that Ireland would find advantage in imperial partnership with England—a revival of Grattan's argument. It should be Irish nationalist policy therefore to placate and join with the imperial power.

In the last years of the nineteenth century the Fenian leaders were mostly old men who had lost their revolutionary drive. There were some exceptions. John Devoy, the head of Clan na Gael in America, for example, indefatigably pushed for the Fenian solution to Ireland's problems—that is, a total rejection of the legitimacy of British rule in Ireland, a rejection to be asserted in arms (to undo not only the Union but, in Fintan Lalor's words, 'the conquest'). Thomas Clarke, an old Fenian who had endured for many years the cruelties of the prison system and had then gone to America, returned to Ireland in 1907 uncompromisingly with the same determination. Meanwhile the British government and parliament had initiated in Ireland (in response to the virtual breakdown of government) what was, in its consequence for the ownership of land, a revolution from above, while a series of committees and commissions and administrative enterprises attempted social and economic reforms whose effect was to take the edge off revolutionary zeal.

But people like Devoy and Clarke encouraged the newcomers who pushed aside the old men of the IRB at the beginning of the new century: young men such as Denis McCullough, Seán Mac Diarmada, Pat McCartan and Ernest Blythe, for example, in Ulster, the province associated in ancient Irish tradition with war and dissension, the centre of nineteenth- and twentieth-century conflict within Ireland.

McCullough at the age of eighteen (in 1901) was sworn into the IRB by his father, and soon proceeded to carry out a purge and reorganization. He in turn swore in Bulmer Hobson and Seán Mac Diarmada. He was co-opted on to the Supreme Council of the IRB and then was director of the organization in Ulster from 1909 to 1916. In 1915 he was elected President of the Supreme Council. Mac Diarmada became national organizer for the IRB in 1908. The old Fenian Tom Clarke was co-opted a member of the Supreme Council in 1909, and Hobson was added in 1911; the Supreme Council was now purged of its more dilatory and cautious members, leaving the activists in full control, including a group which was determined on a rising. Meantime, the IRB took its part in the various 'non-political' movements of the time—the GAA, the Gaelic League, etc.—and set up its own open organizations, such as the Dungannon Clubs, which were involved in the foundation of Sinn Féin.

The Home Rule crisis gave the radicals in the IRB their opportunity: the IRB not only supported the public foundation of the Irish Volunteers in November 1913 (in response to the formation of the Ulster Volunteer Force by Craig and Carson to resist Home Rule) but made every effort to achieve and maintain control of that body. Within weeks Hobson swore Patrick Pearse, one of the founders of the Volunteers, into the IRB. The IRB activists were content that the scholar Eoin MacNeill, who was not one of their number, nor a member of their organization, should head the Volunteers. On 24 April 1914, a cargo of 35,000 rifles, purchased in Germany, was landed at Larne for the Ulster Volunteer Force and quickly distributed throughout Ulster. Meantime, the success of the initial recruitment to the Irish Volunteers alarmed the parliamentary leader John Redmond, since he had no control over this new militia of the people. In June 1914, he asserted his prerogative as the acknowledged leader of nationalist opinion and agitation, and demanded seats for twenty-five nominees of his own on the governing body of the Volunteers—or, he threatened, he would organize a rival force. After some resistance he got his way. Hobson supported the concession to Redmond, and he thereby lost the confidence of Clarke and Mac Diarmada, who opposed it; he resigned from the Supreme Council of the IRB.

From this point there was a division in the IRB and a conspiracy developed within a conspiracy. For there were those who found reason to temporize, and those who were determined to press ahead with insurrection, come what may. Clarke and Mac Diarmada distrusted all compromise in their pursuit of the goal of a rising and resolved to keep their own counsel. On the eve of the Great War small quantities of rifles (1,500 in all) were landed for the Volunteers, mostly at Howth, and were successfully held in spite of efforts by the government to seize them.

When England went to war with Germany and Austria in August 1914, Redmond spoke in the House of Commons in Westminster as leader of Irish nationalism, and assured the British government that it need have no fears about Ireland:

> There are in Ireland two large bodies of Volunteers. One of them sprang into existence in the South. I say to the Government that they may tomorrow withdraw every one of their troops from

Ireland. I say that the coast of Ireland will be defended from foreign invasion by her armed sons, and for this purpose armed Nationalist Catholics in the South will be only too glad to join arms with the armed Protestant Ulstermen in the North. Is it too much to hope that out of this situation there may spring a result which will be good, not merely for the Empire, but for the future welfare and integrity of the Irish nation?

Like so many in Europe that autumn, he saw advantage for his country in the bloody conflict that was now engaged. On 20 September, speaking at Woodenbridge, Co. Wicklow, he went further, and called on his countrymen not merely to defend their own shores but to join in the war on England's side; to commit Ireland against the Central Powers. The original governing body of the Volunteers, headed by MacNeill, rejected this call, and Redmond's followers then seceded, to form a rival body of National Volunteers. Of about 180,000 men, only 11,000, to be known as the Irish Volunteers, remained with MacNeill. Many of the others simply dropped out. The men who went with Redmond, however, were dissipated now. The British refused to allow him to form his Volunteers into an Irish Division, although they allowed an Ulster Division to be formed from the Ulster Volunteer Force, for service in the reorganized British army. There was at the time a prejudice among nationalists against the existing Irish regiments in the regular British army (a prejudice which was not wholly nationalist: there was a class feeling too). Those of Redmond's followers—tens of thousands of them—who answered his call to war joined up as individuals volunteers, and Redmond for the next two years was very active in recruiting for the British army, employing all the high-flown rhetoric, current at the time, that called on men to make a mystical sacrifice of blood:

> It is these soldiers of ours to whose keeping the Cause of Ireland has passed today. It was never in worthier, holier keeping than that of these boys, offering up their supreme sacrifice with a smile on their lips because it was given for Ireland. May God bless them! And may Ireland, cherishing them to her bosom, know how to prove her love and pride and send their brothers leaping to keep full their battle-torn ranks and to keep high and glad their heroic hearts![13]

The Supreme Council of the IRB, meeting in Dublin in 1914, determined to bring about a rising before the war ended and to use the 11,000 Irish Volunteers (of whom they had part control) for this purpose. They made immediate contact with Clan na Gael and in August 1914 John Devoy met Count von Bernstorff, German Ambassador to the United States, in New York, with a request for arms (accompanied by some German officers), to be sent to Ireland. In 1915 a military committee of three—Patrick Pearse, Joseph Plunkett and Éamonn Ceannt—was set up by the Supreme Council to make plans in secret. It worked closely with Mac Diarmada and Clarke. Although McCullough was elected President of the Supreme Council in 1915, he was not kept informed of the military committee's plans. At the end of 1915 or very early in 1916 the final decision was made that the rising should be carried out as soon as possible; they fixed on Good Friday as the date, but within about a month changed this to Easter Sunday. Meantime it became necessary to bring James Connolly, the founder of the Irish Labour Party, into their confidence, for he showed every sign of being about to attempt a rising independently with a much smaller body than the Volunteers, the Irish Citizen Army (a paramilitary organization founded after the police had attacked assemblies of locked-out workers in 1913). These socialists, suspicious of the middle-class leadership of the Volunteers, were also divided in their intentions and purpose; but Connolly himself was more than sympathetic to separatist nationalism, while Pearse, coming relatively lately from cultural to political nationalism, was moving towards a form of socialism. A secret conference was held; Connolly was sworn in and was added to the military council, as was Thomas MacDonagh, who had shown considerable capacity as an organizer in the Volunteers. The seven were now assembled whose names were to be subscribed to the Proclamation. With the aid of Clan na Gael in neutral America contacts had continued with the German government and a shipment of arms from Germany was arranged.

There was an apprehension that Redmond wanted his National Volunteers, ultimately, for fighting the Ulster Volunteer Force if necessary to enforce Home Rule. The Irish Volunteers had a different concept, but they were not wholly under the control of the IRB, and some of the leaders (including MacNeill) were against initiating action against the British but were prepared to fight should any attempt be made to impose conscription on Ireland, to disarm the Volunteers, or to arrest their commanders. The military council therefore strove, in secrecy but with much success, to extend control over the Volunteers and, in particular, to place its own men in regional command, especially in the south-west, where the German arms were to be landed (at Limerick in the initial plans; then at Fenit in Tralee Bay). Plans were prepared for action in three provinces: the military council wished to engage the British, not the Ulster unionists; therefore the Irish Volunteers of Ulster were to march to Connacht, where it was envisaged that a stand, holding the line of the Shannon, could be made. The organizers knew that the chances of military success fell far short of certainty. However, they had sufficient control over the Volunteers, through their infiltration of the governing body, to be confident they could bring them into action; they had the fully committed Citizen Army along with some important trade union facilities (backed by the syndicalist tendencies of Connolly and some of his fellows, which would direct union power, in matters such as the control or disruption of rail and sea transport, to political ends); they had some arms; the German arms shipment, to be augmented by other help, was timed to coincide with the rising; and they felt that they would be able to put up a fight that would electrify the country and astonish the world. Central to their purpose was the proclamation of the sovereignty of the Irish people, maintained by armed force which would make Ireland a belligerent on the side of the Central Powers. The War had gone badly for the Allies in 1915, and the forces of the British empire in particular had suffered disaster in the Dardanelles. Ultimate British defeat was quite possible, and an Irish republic, holding out, perhaps west of the Shannon, with German aid, could conceivably emerge on the winning side. At least, in a negotiated peace, Ireland, as a belligerent, would have its separate place at the conference. The rising, as planned, was not necessarily a forlorn cause. Had the plan, however, gone into effect with even moderate success, it would inevitably have partitioned the country along some ultimate ceasefire line, at least for a time.

The Proclamation was to be printed and widely distributed; it was to be broadcast to the belligerent nations and the whole world (seizure of radio facilities was part of the plan): Ireland's true voice was to be heard. As is well known, all the plans went awry: the arms shipment was tracked and intercepted; MacNeill, hopelessly indecisive and then deceived (partly by an exercise in 'black propaganda' devised by the conspirators), countermanded the order that would have assembled the Volunteers for parades and exercises throughout the country on Easter Sunday: the rising was timed to begin on that Sunday evening. He had been kept in the dark about the details of the intended rising, as indeed had the very President of the Supreme Council himself, Denis McCullough. When the members of the military council, in desperation, decided to bring out what force they could, a day late, on Easter Monday, it was in the knowledge that the rising would now have little or no prospect of military success. It would be a gesture—'propaganda of the deed'. Paradoxically, it is possible that the confusion and failures in the long run served the purposes of the planners better than would successful execution of their preparations. For the British government in Ireland, observing the collapse of the plan, relaxed its vigilance, which had been tense and expectant, and postponed taking action against the would-be insurgents until after the Easter holiday. Having been prepared, it was now taken by surprise, and the insurgents, in spite of all, put up a highly dramatic fight, and their voice was indeed heard.

The purpose of the rising was to issue the Proclamation with sufficient force and courage to give it meaning. The purpose of the Proclamation was to rouse the nation and make it free and independent.

By 1915 the military council, itself an informal and clandestine body within the IRB, was preparing for the likelihood of an uprising: its purpose, what was to be proclaimed, was implicit. The general intention was already clear, and Pearse in particular, the chosen voice of the IRB—since he had the appropriate public presence and gift of words—had already, as it were, rehearsed the declaration of independence in a number of notable speeches and writings. When Connolly was brought into secret conclave with the military council on 19 January 1916, they revealed to him the plans for the rising and co-opted him. No record of the proceedings of the meeting survives; but the general character of the Proclamation *must* have been central to the discussion. Connolly had been pointedly critical of a nationalism that aimed merely at a change of flags. He wanted social revolution and within the week of this secret meeting (which lasted three days) had published his view on the matter.

To this Pearse had already, although fairly recently, been persuaded, as his pamphlet *The Sovereign People* (written just afterwards) illustrates. Like Yeats, he despised the 'filthy modern tide' and the 'fumbling in a greasy till' that the poet saw as the death of 'romantic Ireland'. 'For men were born to pray and save.' He idealized 'the people' and was well on the way, perhaps belatedly, to Connolly's kind of socialism. Connolly was already determined to rise, even with only a few hundred men and women, hoping the Irish Volunteers would then follow that lead, and he was a dedicated nationalist as well as a socialist. From the early days of the war he had shown that he would support the Volunteers *when they were prepared to act*. Compromise between him and Pearse on the statement to be made was probably not difficult, and it is likely that by January, at the latest, the general terms at least of the Proclamation were agreed.

At any rate, when Pearse drafted the final document he incorporated in it Connolly's suggestions, or requirements, with which, it is probable, he was in full agreement. The draft was approved at a meeting on Monday, 17 April 1916, and a Provisional Government decided on.[14] That meeting also approved the circulation of a document purporting to have been issued by Dublin Castle, indicating that the British were about to move against the Volunteers. The Proclamation was finally ratified at a meeting of the military council in Liberty Hall on Easter Sunday, 23 April 1916, and seems to show modifications that reflect the events of the previous few days. All seven signatories were present at the meeting, which began at nine o'clock in the morning. They had to make urgent, fateful and indeed fatal decisions. They knew now that the German arms were lost, intercepted at sea by the British navy two days earlier. MacNeill had published in the Sunday paper his countermanding order cancelling the assemblies of Volunteers for that day which had been intended to begin the rising; the military council had reluctantly endorsed that order, to minimize confusion, and emissaries (including The O'Rahilly) had gone about the country reinforcing the cancellation; so a full muster would now be impossible. They decided to issue new mobilization orders and go ahead anyway, with whatever force could be brought to bear, beginning action at noon the following day.

They now constituted themselves the 'Provisional Government of the Irish Republic'. They elected Pearse President (although in the protocol of the IRB the President of that organization, Denis McCullough, was *ex officio* President of 'the Irish Republic, virtually established') and appointed him Commandant-General of the Irish Republic's forces. These forces, now the 'Army of the Irish Republic', were formed of an amalgamation of the Irish Volunteers, the Irish Citizen Army and a handful of Irish-American 'Hibernian Rifles', with the women's organization, Cumann na mBan and the boys' organization, Na Fianna Éireann, as auxiliaries. Connolly was made Vice-President and Commandant-General of the Dublin Division. The document, the Proclamation, was ready, signed first by Clarke, the senior among them, the old Fenian. Plunkett had called on MacNeill, the leader of the Volunteers, on the previous morning (Saturday)—before the countermanding order was issued—to ask him to sign a proclamation, but MacNeill refused to sign without seeing the document. It was later that day that MacNeill discovered he had been deceived by Plunkett's 'black propaganda' (the forged document purporting to be an order from the Castle to disarm the Volunteers and arrest the leaders) and proceeded to attempt to call off the rising, apparently with success.[15] The seven were now in Connolly's territory—the trade union and Citizen Army headquarters—and Connolly, when the meeting ended, took MacDonagh, with the text, to meet the three compositors who did the printing there, Christopher Brady, Michael Molloy and Bill O'Brien. The three had difficulty, because their equipment was inadequate. The type, a mix of fonts, was deficient in Es; the press was old and in disrepair and it was impossible to maintain even pressure. Working through the night, they produced about 2,500 copies, which on Connolly's orders they gave the following morning to Helena Moloney for distribution. She was a member of the Citizen Army and, having handed out the bundles of the Proclamation, she reported for duty armed with a revolver and took part in the attack on Dublin Castle at noon on Easter Monday.

# On the Text of the Easter Proclamation

## *Poblacht na hÉireann*

This, the heading of the Proclamation, is the only part of the document in the Irish language, if we discount Irish forms of names, of which there are two, 'Seán Mac Diarmada' and 'Éamonn Ceannt'. (Accents are wholly omitted, however.) Two of the signatories, Ceannt and Pearse, were staunch 'Irish Irelanders', to employ a term of the time, and all were sympathetic to the Irish language, so that a greater use of it might have been expected. It may be that the problem of the type excluded it. At that time it was not usual to print Irish in Roman type: a 'Gaelic' font, based on early modern manuscript hands, was commonly employed, but was not available for this document. Certainly the lettering of POBLACHT NA HEIREANN is clumsy and ugly. With the inadequate type mix to hand, it would have been next to impossible to produce an acceptable paragraph or two in Irish.

But it is quite likely that the use of Irish in the body of the Proclamation was not contemplated at all, or at least not given serious consideration. In spite of the intimate associations and mutual influences between the cultural and the radically militant nationalist movements of the time, there remained a sharp distinction between what might be called cultural politics and 'real' politics. The rising was real politics. But it is not as simple as that. The rising was an expression, one of many, of nationalism. Nationalism embodied an affirmation of *difference*. Difference from England, from Great Britain, from the rest of the world, was seen to be manifest in Irish history but above all in cultural history, of which the Irish language, its literature and lore, its modes of expression (and hence modes of thought) and its associated apparatus of metaphor and biorhythm were the plainest evidence. Nationalism, however, also embodied a desire to *belong*—to the world of nation states, to the conformities of modern civilization, to the competition for 'a place in the sun', to the blessed condition, in Emmet's words, 'when my country takes her place among the nations of the earth'. A contradiction required resolution.

The planning and preparation of the rising by an activist group within the IRB had involved propaganda (including anti-recruitment propaganda opposing the British efforts to enlist Irishmen for the battlefields of the Great War) and the careful staging of set-piece shows through which their cause might demonstrate its strength and appeal. Four occasions may be noticed. One was the open politicization of the Gaelic League, which the IRB group had been attempting for some time and which they brought to a conclusion at the League's annual *árd-fheis* in Dundalk in 1915, when Douglas Hyde resigned from the presidency.[16] Pearse was present on the platform but did not speak on this occasion. He was by now opposed to Hyde's policy but greatly admired the man, whom he regarded in many respects as his 'leader'. The politicization of the League reflected the change that was taking place in his own life; for his early interests had been largely educational and cultural; he was dedicated to the salvation, virtually in a religious sense, of Ireland, and was now changing the emphasis of his purpose from the cultivation of the country's identity and soul, towards Tone's declared object, 'to break the connection with England'. The IRB group, while they found attractive both Pearse's platform eloquence and his devotion to an idea of Ireland that well suited their aims, had yet remained suspicious of his apparent openness to compromise on the side of parliamentarianism; but he was changing. He had been associated with the League since its early days and was editor of its paper, *An Claidheamh Solais*. But, having come to the conclusion himself that Ireland could not be saved through the cultivation of the Irish language alone, or through the instillation of Gaelic traditions and values in the young, but only through political organization culminating in a warlike achievement of independence, he decided in retrospect that the 'non-political' Gaelic League had in fact been political in its true purpose all along. The League was the precursor. He wrote:

> ... when the seven men met in O'Connell Street to found the Gaelic League, they were commencing ... not a revolt, but a revolution. The work of the Gaelic League, its appointed work, was that: and the work is done.[17]

Was he beginning, perhaps subconsciously, to conclude that the work of the Irish language—giving form to the Irish soul—was done? Or did he still as fervently believe that Ireland should be 'not merely free, but Gaelic as well'? It was the English form of his name that he signed to what he must have regarded as the most important writing (itself in English) of his life.

On 31 March 1912, a year and a half before he was sworn into the IRB, Pearse had spoken at a great mass meeting in Dublin, assembled to support John Redmond and the Third Home Rule Bill. On this occasion Pearse spoke in Irish. The reasons for choosing to do so were probably mixed. The occasion was that of a rally intended to be representative of all nationalist Ireland, and he would certainly have regarded it as fitting that the country's ancient language, with the cultivation of which he was still closely engaged, and which he and many others hoped would soon again be the spoken tongue of the nation, should be employed at a gathering that possibly heralded the dawn of freedom. But it may be, also, that on this public occasion he was using Irish as the cant of a freemasonry to convey an alternative message. It is plain that he was more than doubtful about the cause to which he was here lending his voice; he had a special audience to whom, by making his speech in Irish, he could speak, as it were, *sotto voce* (I translate his words):

> There are some among us who never bowed head or bent knee in homage to the king of England, and who never will. As everyone knows, I belong to this latter group. But it seems to me that I would betray my people on the very day that battle is joined, had I not answered the call to today's assembly; since it is clear to me that the Bill which has been proposed will be of advantage to the Irish, and that the Irish will be stronger for the fight under this Act than without it ... And, if we are cheated this time, there are those in Ireland—and I am one of them—who will advise the Irish never again to deal and negotiate with the foreigners, but to answer them henceforth with the strong hand and the sword's edge. Let the foreigners understand that if we are betrayed again there will be bloody war throughout Ireland.[18]

Here, it would seem, he was speaking out of the side of his mouth, expressing his distrust of that which he was overtly supporting, and—using the code of the Irish language—communicating to the unreconstructed 'physical force men' that he might, really, be one of them.

Even before he was sworn in as a member of the IRB, the activist inner group of that organization chose him as their voice. The Proclamation was, as it were, first rehearsed when he was the deputed speaker at Wolfe Tone's grave in Bodenstown, Co. Kildare, in June 1913. He spoke in English:

> ... in this sacred place, by this graveside, let us not pledge ourselves unless we mean to keep our pledge—we pledge ourselves to follow in the steps of Tone, never to rest, either by day or by night, until his work be accomplished, deeming it the proudest of all privileges to fight for freedom, to fight, not in despondency, but in great joy, hoping for the victory in our day, but fighting on whether victory seem near or far, never lowering our ideal, never bartering one jot or tittle of our birthright, holding faith to the memory and the inspiration of Tone, and accounting ourselves base as long as we endure the evil thing against which he testified with his blood.[19]

And it was mainly in English that he spoke again at the funeral carefully planned and staged by the IRB group in August 1915. The body of the old Fenian O'Donovan Rossa had been brought back from America, through the agency of Clan na Gael, to be buried in Dublin. For the procession to the cemetery, organized by Thomas MacDonagh, the Irish Volunteers (and the Citizen Army) took over the streets of the city, and at the graveside, Pearse, in Volunteer uniform, delivered his most famous oration. This was in itself a declaration of independence.

We are left then, in the Proclamation, with just three words in Irish. It was addressed to the whole population of the island and, other considerations aside, it intended an ecumenism that transcended Gaelic Ireland. The three words are not without interest in themselves. The Irish language had a reasonably sophisticated political vocabulary, including of course many terms and expressions fitted to the singularities of the old Gaelic order of society. But that order had finally collapsed by the eighteenth century, just when a new political vocabulary was coming into being in the European languages.[20] There was by then no Standard Irish, no established canon (although there had been, virtually up until then) to absorb these new terms in the eighteenth and nineteenth centuries. Those who wanted to translate modern political expressions into Irish either had a choice among gaelicizations or borrowed forms or, sometimes, had to resort to the construction of neologisms.

The word '*poblacht*', a neologism, is a translation. There can be no suggestion that Pearse, or Pearse and Connolly, thought first of the term '*Poblacht na hÉireann*' and from that went on to arrive at the rendering 'the Irish Republic'. It was undoubtedly the other way round. The English word 'republic' in this usage is a modern borrowing from the French '*république*', which in turn derives from the Latin '*res publica*'. It derives doubly from it, for the French word was both revived and fortified by the classicism of the eighteenth century and the French Revolution. The older English word of similar meaning is 'commonweal' or 'commonwealth'. But in the borrowings from language to language and in the usage of current political discourse, meanings shifted. There was, in the early twentieth century, no single word in Irish which must be employed to represent the English word 'republic' in its sense either of 'a State not headed by a monarch' or of 'a State with a democratic or liberal form of government'. T. O'Neill Lane's *Larger English-Irish Dictionary*, first published in Dublin in 1904, gives, in the enlarged and revised version of 1921, two words for 'Republic'—'*poiblidheacht*' and '*comh-fhlaitheacht*'. Patrick S. Dinneen's *Irish-English Dictionary*, also published in Dublin in 1904, has no version of the word '*poblacht*'. For the word '*Cómh-flatheacht*' it gives the meanings: 'a joint sovereignty, a commonwealth, a republic; aristocracy'. The plates of this edition were destroyed in the fires of 1916, but a new edition was published in 1927 and reprinted with additions in 1934. In the 1934 version the word '*poblacht*' appears, with the explanation: 'a republic (recent); cf. *ríoghacht*'.

The word chosen, '*poblacht*', as Dinneen suggests, is analogous to and based on the old word '*ríocht*'— 'kingdom'. It was not in any of its variants current in the Irish language before 1916. It might be rendered 'people-dom'. It served very well therefore to convey both of the current political meanings of 'republic', for 'people-dom' could reasonably translate 'democracy' ('people-government') while at the same time the substitution of '*pobal*' for '*rí*' effectively excluded kingship. Some years later, in 1921, when Éamon de Valéra, President of the Irish Republic reproclaimed in 1919, went to London to negotiate the Anglo-Irish truce of that year:

He handed Mr Lloyd George a document in Irish, and then a translation in English. The Irish document was headed '*Saorstat Eireann*'
and Mr Lloyd George began by asking modestly for a literal translation, saying that 'Saorstat' did not strike his ear as Irish. Mr de
Valera replied 'Free State'. 'Yes', retorted Mr Lloyd George, 'but
what is the Irish word for Republic'. While Mr de Valera and his
colleague were pondering in English on what reply they should
make Mr Lloyd George conversed aloud in Welsh with one of his
Secretaries to the discomfiture of the two Irishmen and as Mr de
Valera could get no further than Saorstat and Free State Mr Lloyd
George remarked 'Must we not admit that the Celts never were
Republicans and have no native word for such an idea.'[21]

'*Ríocht na hÉireann*' or '*Ríocht Éireann*' may have been in Pearse's mind.
It was a term particularly to be associated with the early modern period,
especially the seventeenth century, when the Gaelic world last functioned
as a whole polity and when, under the Stuarts, there were three distinct
kingdoms, of Ireland, Scotland and England, under the one crown. The
Stuarts, by a convenient convention of blood descent, could be regarded
as the legitimate heirs of the ancient high kings of Ireland, and the Four
Masters entitled their protonationalist compilation of chronicles '*Annála
Ríoghachta Éireann*', 'The Annals of the Kingdom of Ireland'. Now, however, the legitimate heir of the high kings was to be 'the People', of
*Poblacht na hÉireann*.

The expression, however, carrying, if it does, that baggage of the past,
is not quite a precise translation of 'the Irish Republic', although it will
pass. It may well be that in the three-word heading of the Proclamation
we already have a reminiscence of some confusion of purpose. Pearse was,
by 1916 at any rate, a republican (in the sense of an aspirant to a state
without a monarch), and would never (as he pointed out in 1912) have
been prepared to accept the king of England, George v, or any member
of his family, as monarch of Ireland. But '*Ríocht na hÉireann*', with an Irish
king, might well have been acceptable, had it been possible to imagine a
restoration in some sense of the Gaelic past of, say, the twelfth century,
when there had been a unified Irish kingdom, sharing in the civilization
of Europe, but with its own language and culture, or if there were available a Hugh O'Neill of Tyrone, who had presided over a later, much
diminished and barbarized, polity, but who had the breeding, education

and presence that made him acceptable in the courts of Spain and Rome as a prince of ancient blood. In the social models he held up to the pupils in his school, St Enda's, Pearse had shown an idealized Ireland of the past (as in his pamphlet on first-century Ireland, based, although somewhat anachronistically, on fact rather than fancy) or Plutarchian examples of classical biography. However, no Cormac mac Cuilennáin or Hugh O'Neill was available. The advent of some agreed German princeling, such as had been supplied for Belgium and Greece in the previous century,[22] would not square with Gaelic yearnings; while the coronation, at Tara perhaps, of a country solicitor or doctor who laid dubious claims to remote royal ancestry, would be merely ridiculous. '*Ríocht na hÉireann*' simply was no longer possible.

The Proclamation, therefore, had to proclaim something comparatively new; not a restoration of the Gaelic past. But something new was not intended, at least by Pearse; rather, the proclamation of a nation that existed, that had continued to exist, in the minds and loyalties of its people, independently, as it were, of its own history of some centuries past. An ingenious evasion was devised for this: the device of non-recognition of the existing polity; and this non-recognition allowed '*Poblacht na hÉireann*' to be proclaimed in the way it was. And for the republic there were canonical precedents. Tone had proclaimed a new union of Gael and Gall under the aegis of a republic. The United Irishmen of 1798 had proclaimed a republic, in Ulster, and again in Connacht. Emmet had proclaimed a republic. The Fenians had announced a republic, 'virtually established', and Pearse and his comrades had sworn the Fenian oath to this tenuous ghost of the ancient, independent, sovereign *Ríocht na hÉireann*. It required a hybrid historical myth, the grafting of the secular ahistorical modernizing new order of Tone onto the royalist Catholic archaizing Gaelic medieval tradition, like grafting a spruce onto an oak; but just such a hybrid had been cultivated by nationalism in the nineteenth century.

### The Provisional Government of the Irish Republic to the People of Ireland

The term 'provisional' resonates in twentieth-century Irish politics. The word is a symptom of instability. It has commonly been self-applied elsewhere by governments, usually military, which have seized dictatorial power by coup but claim to have the intention of returning to a more regular mechanism of succession, at some moment convenient to themselves. The 'Government of the Irish Republic' was not the first provisional government announced in Ireland in this century. The Ulster unionist rebellion against the Home Rule Bill led to the setting up in November 1913 (by the Ulster Unionist Council) of a provisional government for the province.[23] This, however, did not attempt to seize power immediately; it was doubly provisional; it organized, armed, drilled and waited in the wings, ready to strike the moment the Bill was passed, but hopeful of blocking the Bill.

The open debate on Home Rule was superseded in the shaping of political reality by a series of intrigues behind the scenes, involving politicians in Westminster, Whitehall, Dublin and Belfast, the king, the British army in Ireland and in England and, to a lesser extent, representatives or agents of foreign powers. By the end of 1914 it might be said that there were three potential native governments in Ireland: Redmond and the leadership of his party, backed by the National Volunteers, waiting for Westminster to set up a subordinate parliament in Dublin, through which they would hold office; Carson, Craig and the Ulster Unionist Council, backed by the Ulster Volunteer Force, working to prevent Home Rule, but prepared, should it happen, to take independent action and seize power in Ulster; and Clarke, Mac Diarmada and their fellows, backed by the Irish Volunteers, waiting for Home Rule not to happen. When it didn't happen, but instead large numbers of young Irishmen were being recruited into the British army to fight England's war, the potential of the IRB government was realised.

Pearse, it might be said, had stolen Carson's thunder. But it is unlikely that this was his purpose, or the purpose of his colleagues. They were purblind (not wholly blind) to the meaning of Carson and the Ulster unionists. They understood, or at least Pearse understood and Connolly understood, that the Ulster rebellion against Home Rule was a declaration of Irish independence—as indeed it was and continues to be—but they failed to see fully how unamenable Ulster unionist independence was and would be to what they themselves asserted and desired. They thought, or perhaps rather wished to think, that the unionists were in some sense their allies against both the British and the Irish parliamentarians, and they had at least half persuaded themselves at the same time that Carson's followers were dupes of the British, deceived into separation from the Irish nation to which they of right belonged, who could in due course be brought to their true allegiance. If the 'provisional government' of 1916 was inspired by the 'provisional government' of 1913, it was in this sense.

But, bearing in mind that this document was drafted by Pearse, we must look to another precedent. Robert Emmet was one of Pearse's heroes and exemplars. Emmet too had issued a Proclamation, in 1803, which set up a provisional government in Dublin (an absurdity, both in its actuality and in its outcome, in the face of real state power—and this was galling to the admirer of Emmet). We can be certain that Emmet was in Pearse's mind when he was chosen by the IRB military council to be President of the Provisional Government of the Irish Republic in 1916. He revered him, as did a great many Irish people, in town and country, throughout the later nineteenth century, and it is clear from his writings that he could envisage no higher destiny than to follow in Emmet's footsteps. And the form of words employed in this heading of the Proclamation follows Emmet exactly:

> The Provisional Government to the People of Ireland
> You are now called upon to show the world that you are competent to take your place among nations; that you have a right to claim their cognizance of you as an independent country, by the only satisfactory proof you can furnish of your capability of maintaining your independence—your wresting it from England with your own hands ... . Our object is to establish a free and independent republic in Ireland ...[24]

The new state being proclaimed was not 'the Republic of Ireland' (which would be the obvious translation of '*Poblacht na hÉireann*') but 'the Irish Republic'. This may seem an over-subtle distinction; but it is one rooted in revolutionary history. 'The French Republic' ('*La République Française*') is sharply distinct, verbally, from 'the Kingdom of France'. France is the royal estate belonging to the king of France. The French Republic is the state constituted by the French. The very title signified a transfer of power.

The Easter document, by proclaiming both '*Poblacht na hÉireann*' and 'the Irish Republic', to some extent falls between the two stools. The hybrid myth shows a weakness at the point of graft. There is an element of ambiguity, but the body of the Proclamation shows that the ambiguity had already begun to be resolved by the time of the rising; the traditional abstract was already yielding to the modernist concrete; the often personified but essentially abstract 'Ireland' of the imagined past was, to some extent at least, being superseded by actual, living and breathing people, the Irish. Buried in this ambiguity was the possibility that 'the Irish Republic' was not necessarily of the same scope as 'the Republic of Ireland'—a distinction which has become very clear to unionists.

But this second, English-language, heading of the Proclamation begs another question. According to it, the government of a state is issuing this statement, the 'provisional government' of the Irish Republic. And the implication of the ensuing document is that there is and has been a real state, but that up to this moment circumstances have deprived the state of a government. Now that the state has been activated, aroused from the sleep of ages, a government must be provided and inserted into a regrettable gap in the arrangements. How is the gap to be filled, 'provisionally' and, by implication, temporarily?

The antecedents of the Irish Republic go back to the proclamations of the United Irishmen (including Robert Emmet); but the 1916 rising was planned by a group within the IRB, and the concept they had of the independent Irish state derived directly from the ideas on the matter, such as they were, of the Fenians. Some leading Fenians (John O'Leary, for example) were not republicans and never took the Fenian oath. The IRB seems to have been originally the 'Irish Revolutionary Brotherhood' rather than the 'Irish Republican Brotherhood'; but the whole tendency of the movement was radically republican and democratic. It came under the influence of Civil War America (and in particular of the ideology of the victorious Union after 1865) and of both republican and Bonapartist ideas in mid-nineteenth-century France. The Fenian oath gave expression to what became the intentions of the revitalized IRB of the early twentieth century. Its wording was as follows:

> I, A.B., in the presence of Almighty God, do solemnly swear allegiance to the Irish Republic, now virtually established; and that I will do my utmost, while life lasts, to defend its independence and integrity; and, finally, that I will yield implicit obedience in all things not contrary to the laws of God, to the commands of my superior officers. So help me God![25]

This superseded an earlier version and was the 'Paris' form of the oath, devised by James Stephens and Thomas Clarke Luby in that city in 1859.

Luby, testifying to O'Leary many years later, confessed that his memory was uncertain and that the original form of words may have read 'not contrary to the laws of morality' rather than 'not contrary to the laws of God'. This suggested alternative is probably correct, since the model for Fenian republicanism, both indirectly, through the tradition of the United Irishmen of the late eighteenth century, and directly, through their contacts with European liberals and revolutionaries, was that of French secular republicanism.

At any rate, this oath embodied an idea very pertinent to the Proclamation. It is said that Stephens was very pleased with the formula, 'the Irish Republic, now virtually established'. It was indeed an ingenious device, because it begged some awkward questions. It called on the novice Fenian to swear soldierly allegiance to a state already existing, in legitimacy if not in dominion; he was not being sworn in as a rebel against God or against lawful human authority, but as the servant of his country, whose apparatus of independent and sovereign government was only temporarily invisible or in abeyance.

Another aspect of the oath was that it superseded merely local and particular grievance, and distanced the Fenian organization from the oath-bound rural secret societies and agitations with which it (like the United Irish societies of the late eighteenth century) was closely connected in origin or context. Such societies, like their kind throughout the world, tended to present their case as that of people driven by intolerable grievance to resort to force not against their lawful king but against his evil advisers and ministers who oppressed his subjects without his knowledge or contrary to his wishes. The early resolutions of the United Irishmen employ this argument at times:

> By Liberty we never understood unlimited freedom, nor by Equality the levelling of property, or the destruction of subordination.—This is a calumny invented by that faction or that gang which misrepresents the King to the People, and the People to the King, traduces one half of the nation to cajole the other, and by keeping up distrust and division, wishes to continue the proud arbitrators of the fortune and fate of Ireland.[26]

There is an element of such argument in the American Declaration of Independence, although that document proceeded to a rejection of the king, holding him responsible in the end for the failure to redress the colonials' recited grievances; however, the previous legitimacy of his rule was acknowledged. And such societies were formed to right local and particular wrongs, and were local and particular in their allegiance, as is illustrated in a Whiteboy oath:

> I do hereby solemnly and sincerely swear, that I will not make known any secret now given me, or that hereafter may be given me, to any one in the world, except a sworn person belonging to the society called *White-boys*, or otherwise, *Sive Ultagh's children*. Furthermore I swear, that I will be ready at an hour's warning (if possible) being properly summoned by any of the officers, serjeants, or corporals belonging to my company. Furthermore I swear, that I will not wrong any of the company I belong to, of the value of one shilling; nor suffer it to be done by others, without acquainting them thereof ...[27]

The point about the Fenian oath is that it pledged allegiance to a much larger polity and that, by silent implication, it denied that the queen of England had or ever had had any legitimate authority over Ireland, whose people owed allegiance only to—what had at the time no manifest machinery of authority—their country. As in the French Declaration of the Rights of Man and of the Citizen, sovereignty resided in 'the Nation'. The oath was republican, partly at least, *faute de mieux*; there was no Irish king, 'virtually established' or otherwise, to whom the Irish owed their loyalty. The only viable alternative at that time was Queen Victoria (to whom, of course, many Irish nationalists who were not outright separatists were prepared to give allegiance).

The Republic's Provisional Government had established itself in the centre of Dublin. The plans for the rising had called for insurrection throughout three provinces and had envisaged the possible loss of Ireland east of the Shannon to the enemy, but the continuance of resistance in the west. It must be remembered that at Easter 1916 the victory of the Central Powers seemed quite possible, and many thought it likely. (In the outcome, it was the entry of the United States into the war in 1917, with the subsequent deployment of American troops in Europe, that was to swing the balance against Germany and Austria just when those nations had, barely, established military superiority over the European Allies.) Victory, in alliance with the Central Powers, was therefore a possibility for the rising; and a government functioning, not merely for a time, but permanently, in the west was consonant with Fenian thinking of the previous century. Some Fenians, reflecting a widespread hostile feeling towards Dublin as the centre of British rule in Ireland, had suggested a somewhat decentralized government for the independent republic, functioning in Athlone, the geographical centre of the island, and in Limerick, on the Shannon, at the head of the estuary that flows westward and faces America. However, since the original plans for the rising had gone so badly awry, the 1916 Provisional Government was in fact in Dublin, indeed virtually confined to Dublin in its operations, and from then on no significant suggestion was made that Ireland's capital city should be elsewhere.[28] Pearse and Connolly in any case were last-minute Fenians, whose thoughts had not been formed in rural Fenian moulds. Pearse was a Dublinman and it was his desire to redeem his native city from 'many shames' and exalt it among Irish places just as Ireland was to be exalted among the nations. Connolly was an urban socialist (born in Edinburgh) whose strong romantic streak was not sufficient for him to be attracted to fantasies of a capital city in a market town or on the Hill of Tara, or the like. Both, although in different ways, had grappled with the modern world as well as with traditions and imaginings of the past. Both were busy and practical men, who clearly discerned the priorities of their lives and had some understanding of the limitations of their aspirations.

The American Declaration of Independence is addressed to 'the opinions of Mankind': it is a manifesto to the world. The French Declaration of the Rights of Man and of the Citizen (like the English Declaration of Rights of a hundred years earlier) is essentially addressed to the king, to inform him of the terms of the social contract and that his absolute right to rule is now denied and ended. The Easter Proclamation is addressed to 'the people of Ireland'. It is appealing to them over the heads of all existing representative assemblies and governmental systems. Since the phrase 'people of Ireland' recurs in the Proclamation, we have sufficient context to infer that 'people' here is in intention a concrete plural rather than an abstract singular; not 'the People' ('*das Volk*') but simply 'people'. It is the equivalent of addressing the citizens of the Irish Republic, 'now virtually established', and indicates that its authors, undoubtedly nationalists, were also humanists. Although it had been planned to publish the Proclamation throughout the world, and although this publication was a prime purpose of the rising, yet the document, in its form, is not the equivalent of the public announcement of a birth, a marriage, or a divorce; rather, it is in the nature of a communication from the head of a family to its members. This is reinforced by the references in the text to 'children', references which, in one case at least, have caused some later confusion. It is Ireland, the mother, who is addressing her family.

## 2. THE FIRST PARAGRAPH

### Irishmen and Irishwomen

The preceding heading is 'To the people of Ireland'. The opening address of the main text spells this out: it calls on 'Irishmen and Irishwomen'. Two things are to be noticed first about it: its ecumenical intent and its relevance to the women's suffrage movement which had been so much to the fore in British, and to an extent in Irish, politics up to the beginning of the Great War.

Pearse in his earlier writings had emphasized the centrality, as he saw it, of the Gaelic tradition in Ireland. He refers frequently to the history, the sufferings, the endurance, the nobility of 'the Gael'. In Irish there is a distinction between '*Éireannach*' (an Irish person, a person born and brought up in Ireland) and '*Gael*' (a person of the old stock and culture that had existed in Ireland before the advent of Danes, Normans and English). The distinction, which had cultural and social meaning in the late Middle Ages and the early modern period, was all but meaningless in the twentieth century in historical terms (except insofar as the native speakers of Irish in the west and south might be reasonably deemed to continue, in however attenuated a tradition, an ancient polity), but it had been given a new meaning not only by the revivalist movements but by the racial stereotyping and social-Darwinian prejudices of the day. On at least one occasion Pearse had had to defend himself against the charge of being a 'Palesman addressing the mere Gael'. To be a Gael over and above being an Irishman or Irishwoman had however become a matter of choice, and to a considerable extent a matter of self-delusion. It was to identify with a fairly remote past and, more importantly, to reject much of the present. There was a strong case to be made for so doing. The present was disagreeable to Irish people of sensibility and the attempt to invent an identity was moderately successful.

The distinction had been brought sharply to the fore in the pages of the *Nation* by Thomas Davis, who exhibits remarkable ambiguity on the subject. For he attempted on the one hand to support the view of Wolfe Tone and abolish the distinctions between Catholic, Protestant and Dissenter (that is, between ancient native and historic settler traditions) in favour of 'the common name of Irishman'; while on the other hand he showed flashes of contempt and intolerance for the language, traditions and culture of the 'Anglo-Saxons'. The ambiguity was to persist as a dichotomy between the emphases of cultural nationalism and the emphases of political nationalism two or three generations later. Racial and cultural prejudice was a feature of the dominant Western imperialism of the late-nineteenth- and early twentieth-century period, and the cult of the 'Gael' was in part a response to the bitter and irrational ethnic and racial assertions of English power throughout the empire, and in particular those of the ruling class. It proved to be a very powerful response. But it continued to impale separatist nationalists on the horns of a dilemma. Terence MacSwiney, then a Volunteer officer and organiser in Cork (and, in the original plan for the rising, designated a leader in that city), was struggling with the question, as he shows in an article collected in his *Principles of Freedom*:

It is well, then, that the unconvinced Gall should hear why he should accept the Irish language; not simply to defer to the Gael, but to quicken the mind and defend the territory of what is now the common country of the Gael and Gall ... In the widening future that beckons to us, we shall, if anything, give greater praise to these good fighters and enthusiasts, who in darker years, even with the language of the enemy, resisted his march and held the gap for Ireland.

On this ground the Gael and Gall stand on footing of equality ... Some Irishmen not of Gaelic stock speak of Irish as foreign to them, and would maintain English in the principal place now and in the future. We do well then to make clear to such a one that he is asked to adopt the language for Ireland's sake as a nation and for his own sake as a citizen. If he wishes to serve her he must stand for the language; if he prefers English civilisation he should go back to England ... So the Irishman of other than Gaelic ancestors should stand in with us, not accepting something disagreeable as inevitable, but claiming a right by birth and citizenship, joining the fine army of the nation for a brave adventurous future, full of fine possibility and guaranteed by a fine comradeship—owning a land not of flattery and favouritism, but of freedom and manhood. This saving ideal has often been obscured by our sundering class names. That is why we would substitute as common for all the fine name of Irishman.[29]

However, it was also to 'Irishmen' that Redmond consistently appealed in his urgings to show Irish worthiness of a share in empire through willingness to join up and fight in the war. And it was, now, to 'Irishmen' (and 'Irishwomen') that Pearse and his fellows addressed their Proclamation. As is clear from the continuing text, Pearse and Connolly, here, were intending (as a matter of principle rather than practical discourse) to include 'Orangemen' (and 'Orangewomen', if such may be imagined)[30] in their call to arms. It is important too that the vocative, 'Irishmen!' had significant precedents: so Humbert and McCracken and Sheares had opened their proclamations: it is a direct and levelling, a republican, address, and by its very meaning nationalist.

'Irishmen and Irishwomen!' The hand of Connolly, almost certainly, is to be seen in the inclusiveness here. It is not that Pearse didn't allow women a place in the Ireland of his dreams: far from it. But their place in his writings was, above all, as mothers, who must offer up sons (to the cause of the motherland) and who must otherwise be sheltered and protected as the sex created to give life and to provide the chaste example of passive sacrifice. Pearse revered women, very much as they were theoretically revered by the public morality of the British society of his day; his reverence expected of them the strength to endure, to sacrifice and to suffer. A women's organization, Cumann na mBan, was associated with the Volunteers. It was an organization of non-combatant auxiliaries, serving the men, something like the Voluntary Aid Detachment which supplied amateur nurses, ambulance drivers, stenographers and messengers to the British army, in Dublin as well as in France and Flanders.

For Connolly's different romanticism, women were comrades, friends, mothers, wives and daughters; side by side with the men in the struggle for existence. There were women soldiers in the Citizen Army, armed and active, most notably Countess Markievicz, who fought in St Stephen's Green, eager to bag her man early on, like a novice proving himself on a grouse shoot. Pearse, in this as in other matters, was coming round to a view close enough to Connolly's. It may be noted in passing that Seán

O'Casey, who had been quarrelling with the Citizen Army (of which he was secretary), partly because of its new intimacy with the petty-bourgeois Volunteers and the IRB, and who was to comment on the Rising and its consequence through his plays, was closer to Pearse's and the conventional middle-class view of women in society (highly sentimentalized in his case): in his plays women were the virtuous chorus of commonsense and of devotion to life, pure and noble souls, while the men, socialist, republican, Orange, Green or Red, were the foolish and knavish protagonists engaging in a dance of death.

*In the name of God and of the dead generations from which she receives her old tradition of nationhood, Ireland, through us, summons her children to her flag and strikes for her freedom.*

The Americans, in their Declaration of Independence, appealed to 'the Supreme Judge of the World' for the rectitude of their intention; the French in 1789 made their Declaration 'in the presence' and under the auspices of the Supreme Being. The Americans were making their solemn declaration in the form of an oath, calling on God to witness that they spoke truth; that is, that their intentions were pure and honest. The French went somewhat beyond this, offering the Supreme Being not only as a witness but as a patron of their declaration—since, after all, it was being made in accordance with the precepts of reason and must therefore be, in a sense, divinely inspired.

The Irish proclamation goes beyond solemnity. These opening words, clearly intended not only to be momentous but to overwhelm with the awful grandeur of the moment, hover on the brink of bathos. It is Pearse's sense of style that is all but overwhelmed. Where the Americans had made their declaration to the world 'in the Name, and by the Authority, of the good People of these Colonies'—exaggerating their empowerment somewhat (their delegated discretion had arguably been usurped by caucuses and street committees), but still calling upon an authority which, by reasonable procedures, had been vested in them—the authors of the Proclamation here represent 'Ireland', agent of God *and* of history—of the dead—as calling her children to arms. It is a strictly apostolic form of address: 'she' is passing on God's message as handed down by an inspired tradition; but there is an imbalance arising from a misjudgment of context: here, inadvertently, it is God who is made the agent of a political opinion.

Although like most such documents the Proclamation is commonly little read in detail, two phrases from it have passed into Irish popular memory, and this is one of them. It surfaces mainly as a parody or a jibe. It is not the assumption of divine authority that causes the embarrassment giving rise to this; it is the 'dead generations'. *Liebestod* tends to make the unromantic uneasy. (The other remembered phrase, often misattributed to the 1937 Constitution, is 'cherishing all the children of the nation equally'.)

The words here are certainly Pearse's rather than Connolly's, and he has condensed into them, perhaps carelessly or hastily, several of his persistently imperative themes: Ireland as the beloved of God; Ireland as mother; the mother as nurturer of warriors and heroes; the long witness of blood offered generation after generation; the martyrs' procession from scaffold to scaffold down the years. There are echoes. Of the words Thucydides put in the mouth of Pericles:

> I shall begin with our ancestors: it is both just and proper that they should have the honour of the first mention on an occasion like the present. They dwelt in the country without break in the succession from generation to generation, and handed it down free to the present time by their valour ...[31]

Of Lincoln's First Inaugural:

> The mystic chords of memory, stretching from every battlefield and patriot grave, and to every living heart and hearthstone, all over this broad land, will yet swell the chorus of the Union, when again touched, as surely they will be, by the guardian angels of our nature.[32]

And of Pearse's own graveside orations, the panegyrics on Tone and on O'Donovan Rossa.

It may be, and it probably was, that he intended 'In the name of God' to be no more than the invocation of a blessing on an undertaking (as 'In the name of God, let us begin'); but, if so, he was carried away by the effort at solemnity: this is not quite what the chosen form of words says. The words are a call to a jihad; the Irish people are being summoned to war in the name of God and of the nation's martyrs. The authors of the

Proclamation have now distanced themselves (although under the aegis of the general heading, 'the Provisional Government ... to the people of Ireland'). The sense of a government addressing the citizens, adumbrated in the heading of the Proclamation, is now gone. It is not *by* but *through* the Provisional Government that the call to arms is being issued. It is issued *by* a personified Ireland, who in turn is speaking in the name of God and of the dead generations from which *she* (Ireland) receives her old '*tradition* of nationhood' (nationhood as a teaching or a secret that has been handed down the generations). And it is issued to her children, the children of the nation, '*enfants de la patrie*'. ('*Le jour de gloire est arrivé.*')

The ideas embedded in this are simple; but they are brought together into a complexity. The complexity results from an evasion. The authors of the Proclamation most certainly believed that they were not only justified in what they were doing in bringing about the rising, but that they were bound to do it. They were all fully prepared to take responsibility for their action, and they did so. But they were trying to straddle a chasm, between heroic myth and the banal practicalities of early twentieth-century liberal politics. They were at one and the same time ceremonially offering themselves on a sacrificial altar, and putting forward a practical progamme, like any workaday political party. While they knew themselves to have been chosen—by destiny?—to proclaim the republic, they had few personal credentials to present. The oath they had sworn was secret. Most of them were little known to the Irish public. They hadn't the endorsement of the elected political leaders of nationalist Ireland, of the appointed leadership of the Volunteers, or even of the supreme leadership of the IRB. They spoke on behalf of and at the behest of 'Ireland'. They had to evade all question in the mundane matters of delegation and deputation of power and legitimacy from the everyday world and, although their ultimate purpose lay in that world, they must first speak with the authority of the Birds of Cloudcuckooland addressing imperial Athens:

> O suffering mankind,
>> lives of twilight,
>>> race feeble and fleeting,
>> like the leaves scattered!
>>> Pale generations,
>>>> creatures of clay,

the wingless, the fading!
   Unhappy mortals,
      shadows in time,
flickering dreams!
    Hear us now,
      the ever-living Birds,
the undying,
    the ageless ones,
      scholars of eternity.[33]

It is Ireland, female and no doubt in this moment beautiful, who summons her children to her flag and bids them strike for freedom. She is ultimately the sovereignty goddess, the divine and maternal personage of many names—Éire, Banba, Fódhla, Clíona, Scáth, Médhbh, Áine, Danu, the Black Rose, the Sweet Brown Cow, the Poor Old Woman, older, as Pearse had written in his verse, than the Nun of Beare, Cathleen ní Houlihan, Yeats's 'young girl, and she had the walk of a queen'.

The flag is not part of that mythology, nor is her 'freedom'. What the old goddess sought was her lover, to lie with her and enjoy kingship—for a night. The lover had been, in the last stage of the history of that imagery, the Stuart king 'over the water'. The flag brings back the twentieth century, or rather the nineteenth, to the imagery. Delacroix had depicted the goddess with the flag, bare-breasted Liberty on the barricade. But was the Ireland of the Proclamation holding a republican tricolour? Or was she like her cousin Brittania, an Athena borrowing war-gear from the gods, sitting enthroned with Poseidon's trident in one hand, in the other Zeus's aegis, decorated with her patriotic blazon?

An interesting question suggests itself here. The late G.A. Hayes-McCoy examined the question of the 1916 flags. He quotes Pearse, in his capacity as Director of Organisation of the Irish Volunteers, issuing an order to units on 10 March 1915:

> Every Company of the Irish Volunteers is to provide itself with an Irish Flag ... The authorised flag is a plain gold harp on a green ground, and no other flag, except authorised regimental colours, is to be carried by bodies of Irish Volunteers. Companies should be exercised in saluting the flag ... Each Company which has not yet done so will take immediate steps to provide itself with a National Flag.[34]

Connolly arranged an elaborate ceremony at Liberty Hall on 16 April 1916, at which Molly Reilly, of the Irish Women Workers' Union, hoisted (in Connolly's words) 'the Green Flag of Ireland, emblazoned with the Harp without the crown, the sacred emblem of Ireland's unconquered soul', which was assigned a colour guard of sixteen men of the Citizen Army and was formally saluted.

This had precedents. The proclamation drafted for the United Irishmen in 1798 by John Sheares, and anticipating their seizure of Dublin, read, in part:

> Irishmen—
> Your country is free and you are about to be avenged. That vile Government, which has so long and so cruelly oppressed you, is no more ... The National Flag, the sacred Green, is at this moment flying over the ruins of Despotism, and that Capital, which a few hours past witnessed the debauchery, the plots and crimes of your Tyrants, is now the citadel of triumphant virtue and patriotism ...[35]

During the Rising, as Hayes-McCoy has established, it may be that three flags flew at the insurgent headquarters, the GPO: a large green flag bearing the painted words (in 'Gaelic' letters, done in yellow and white) 'Irish Republic', which flew at the south end of the O'Connell Street front of the building; a tricolour, with vertical divisions of green, white and orange, which flew at the north end of the O'Connell Street facade; and, possibly, from a third flagstaff at the centre of the building, on the roof, the green flag with the golden harp (the only evidence for the presence of this third flag is the recollection of Seán T. O'Kelly). A tricolour flew from the College of Surgeons in Saint Stephen's Green (occupied by the Citizen Army), a tricolour (probably) from Jacobs' factory, a green flag with a harp from the Ringsend Road distillery, a tricolour of green, white and orange arranged horizontally (the orange at the top), from the Mendicity Institute, a 'green flag' from the South Dublin Union, a green flag with a harp from the Marrowbone Lane distillery, a green flag with a harp from Liberty Hall and the Starry Plough of Labour and the Citizen Army (a yellow plough, studded with silver stars in the form of the constellation *Ursa Major*, on a field of green) from the Imperial Hotel in Sackville Street.

Up to that moment, the tricolour was not regarded, apparently by anybody, as the national flag. It had not been the flag of the Fenians, the IRB, the Volunteers, or the Citizen Army. Although it was not the Fenian flag it appears by the turn of the century to have become the symbol of radical or republican nationalism, and in April 1901, at the funeral of James Stephens, his coffin 'was wrapped in the Irish Republican flag of white, green and orange'.[36] Its combination of colours seems to have appeared first in 1830, not as a flag but as a favour or cockade, symbolizing an attempt at reconciling Ireland's different traditions, and stimulated by the restoration of the French tricolour in that year by Louis Philippe, when he dethroned Charles X. A green-white-and-orange flag, in French silk, was presented by Thomas Francis Meagher to the chairman of a *soirée* organized jointly by the Loyal National Repeal Association and the Confederate Club (Young Ireland) in April 1848, to welcome Meagher and William Smith O'Brien back from France. But this tricolour was seen only rarely and sporadically in the decades that followed. However—again more commonly as a favour, hatband or armband than as a flag—the combination of the three colours had begun to appear in the period before the rising, not so much as an emblem of Ireland but as an indication of radical—or *republican*—nationalism, just as the Starry Plough (originally on a green field) was an indication of socialism. Yet, it is plain that in the preparations for the rising, tricolour flags were made, and it seems that the one most associated with them was Mac Diarmada.

It is not at all certain that the traditional green flag of nationalist Ireland, bearing 'the harp without the crown', flew over the Post Office, at least on the Monday of Easter Week. The direct evidence that it did is O'Kelly's much later recollection. The indirect evidence is that, if there were no flag on the central staff, then precedence was given to the plain green flag with the words 'Irish Republic', which flew at the south end of the Post Office facade (heraldic right), which seems unlikely given that the leaders were punctilious about flags. But if it did not, it may be due to a mishap: there is some evidence that flags were inadvertently left behind in Liberty Hall at the beginning of the Rising. A large green flag, with a harp, damaged by fire, was found in the ruins of Liberty Hall after Easter Week: it may have been intended for the GPO. It does in any case seem certain that this was regarded by the insurgents as the national flag. Therefore, it must be the flag to which Ireland, in the Proclamation, was summoning her children.

With the crown (and originally blue rather than green), it had been the banner of the kingdom of Ireland since Henry VIII's time, and, with the crown, it was still the emblem of Ireland within the United Kingdom. The red saltire of St Patrick (originally probably the Geraldine blazon), excavated from fairly obscure usages at the end of the eighteenth century—because it would fit onto St Andrew's saltire in the Union flag, graphically, neatly and aesthetically—was its chief rival, rejected, however, by most nationalists. But there is an interesting detail to be noted. Pearse's order to the Irish Volunteers, quoted above, specified a 'plain harp'. This is contrary to what had been laid down by the Provisional Committee of the Volunteers in May 1914 (before the Redmondites had moved in) which had specified a green flag with a gilt harp with a forepillar of a winged maiden, and nine silver strings. The barebreasted winged maiden had appeared, under the crown, on the banners of the Volunteers of 1780 and, without the crown, but frequently with a Cap of Liberty, on the banners and proclamations of the United Irishmen. She was, indeed, held to represent Ireland in herself. The Volunteers of 1913, having appointed a consultative committee of antiquaries to advise on flag design, had originally settled on the winged maiden harp for the national flag. F.J. Bigger was one of those consulted; The O'Rahilly was a principal designer of Volunteer flags, and he took the advice of Dr George Sigerson on this matter, recommending the harp which included the 'figure of Erin' (a harp identified as the 'mystic harp of Dagda'). But this form of the harp was objected to, as being 'probably of foreign rather than Irish origin'. Hayes-McCoy, whose researches revealed this, does not comment further. 'Foreign', however, in much of the nationalist writing of the time, is a code word: the objection to the maiden form of the harp was probably prudish. At any rate, the plain harp prevailed—until 1916. Sigerson, incidentally, later wrote:

> There is a general misunderstanding as to the crownless harp. Some think it an emblem of republicanism, in reality it meant that Ireland had been discrowned as a sovereign power. See Lord Cloncurry's memoirs.[37]

After the rising, of course, the tricolour was to displace the green flag; but that had not happened when the Proclamation was written.

The opening sentence of the Proclamation makes a second statement about what Ireland is doing: she summons her children to her flag, and she 'strikes for her freedom'. The two words, 'strikes' and 'freedom' compress a history and beg a question. To take the second word first, it must be read to mean that at this moment Ireland is not free; it was therefore necessary to 'strike' for freedom. But it could be argued that Ireland was freer than most countries in the world of 1916. Irish adult males were entitled to vote in general elections, reasonably frequently held, and to send to Westminster more than a hundred Members of Parliament. There was a separate Irish executive (with its headquarters in Dublin Castle) and the king was represented in Dublin by a viceroy. There was a system of local government with devolved powers. There was a legal system in place, with trial by jury, and (in theory) restraint on the police power. At least one sizeable section of the population believed itself already free but feared that its freedom was threatened by Home Rule, which was described in an oratorical moment by Carson as 'the most nefarious conspiracy that has ever been hatched against a free people'.[38]

But Home Rule had been voted for three times by the Irish electorate, and had been denied three times in Westminster. The third denial was represented as no more than a postponement for the duration of the war; but there were many who regarded this as a cheat and a fraud, another trick of 'perfidious Albion'. And the war itself had changed things, binding the Irish into a great and bloody conflict, the purpose of which, discarding propaganda, was most obscure but was in any case no concern of theirs. Many Irish people believed that they were not free; that those goods which they most sought—in particular, national independence—would always be denied them by a combination of British force and British deceit and trickery. Franchised or no, they were unwilling subjects of the British empire, like the peoples of India, Burma, Egypt or Rhodesia. And the restraints and protections of law had been often suspended—by a series of Coercion Acts, applicable to Ireland, throughout the nineteenth century, for example, or by the current wartime Defence of the Realm Act. There was the widespread conviction among many Irish people at home and abroad that genocide had been attempted by Britain in Ireland, notably at the time of the Great Famine of the 1840s. A majority of people in the country did not wish to be under British rule, and apprehended that their wish had been repeatedly thwarted. 'Freedom' was their goal.

The word 'strike' is imprecise, but conveys a sense of violent action. It is repeated in the second paragraph of the Proclamation, discussed below: 'she strikes in full confidence of victory'. The Proclamation is primarily a declaration of war; secondarily a declaration of independence: the war is to lead to the independence. This is wholly within its logic, a logic convoluted perhaps, but quite astutely reasoned. It is a declaration of war, not presenting itself as the uprising of an oppressed people against intolerable conditions but as the free act of a sovereign state: by such a free act freedom will be both affirmed and attained. There is no recital of grievances; for there has been no seeking of a right of petition. The Proclamation does not announce that British rule must end because it had been unfair, unjust or oppressive. It declares it at an end because it had no legitimacy. It declares that Ireland, under its rightful government, is entering the Great War on the side of the Central Powers and against the Allies, but specifically, of course, against England. (There is, however, throughout the document, no naming of enemy or ally, but, as will be seen, the import is clear.)

The Proclamation is, amongst other things, the direct response to Redmond's Woodenbridge speech, in which he had attempted to commit Ireland to the English cause. Now, according to the members of the Provisional Government, Ireland, through them, is answering him. The writer James Stephens (a friend of Thomas MacDonagh), who witnessed the Rising and wrote a reminiscence of his observations of that Easter Week, discerned this meaning, and saw in Redmond's folly the immediate cause of what he had witnessed:

> It happened because the leader of the Irish Party misrepresented his people in the English House of Parliament. On the day of the declaration of war between England and Germany he took the Irish case, weighty with eight centuries of history and tradition, and he threw it out of the window. He pledged Ireland to a particular course of action, and he had no authority to give this pledge and he had no guarantee that it would be met. The ramshackle intelligence of his party and his own emotional nature betrayed him and us and England. He swore Ireland to loyalty as if he had Ireland in his pocket, and could answer for her. Ireland has never been disloyal to England, not even at this epoch, because she has never been loyal to England, and the profession of her national faith has been unwavering, has been known to every English person alive, and has been clamant to all the world beside.[39]

## 3. THE SECOND PARAGRAPH

*Having organised and trained her manhood through her secret revolutionary organisation, the Irish Republican Brotherhood, and through her open military organisations, the Irish Volunteers and the Irish Citizen Army, having patiently perfected her discipline, having resolutely waited for the right moment to reveal itself, she now seizes that moment ...*

'Ireland' did all this. It is still the personified Nation in action. This short but measured period—undoubtedly consisting of Pearse's words—is drama. We have here, with some inversions, an echo of, or rather the denouement led up to by, Pearse's oration at the grave of O'Donovan Rossa. Having given the oration at that funeral, he now explicates. The patriot dead have been invoked, and that invocation gives benediction now to the resolve of the patriot living.

The panegyric on O'Donovan Rossa was to some extent modelled on Lincoln's Gettysburg Address, as that in turn was to some extent modelled on the funeral speech of Pericles.[40] Lincoln's famous speech was short enough to be given here in full:

> Four score and seven years ago our fathers brought forth on this continent a new nation, conceived in Liberty, and dedicated to the proposition that all men are created equal.
>
> Now we are engaged in a great civil war, testing whether that nation or any nation so conceived and so dedicated can long endure. We have come to dedicate a portion of that field as a final resting place for those who here gave their lives that the nation might live.
>
> But in a larger sense we cannot dedicate—we cannot consecrate—we cannot hallow—this ground. The brave men, living and dead, who struggled here, have consecrated it, far above our poor power to add or detract. The world will little note nor long remember what we say here, but it can never forget what they did here. It is for us the living, rather, to be dedicated here to the unfinished work which they who fought here have thus far so nobly advanced. It is rather for us to be here dedicated to the great task remaining before us—that from these honoured dead we take increased devotion to that cause for which they gave the last full measure of devotion—that we here highly resolve that these dead

LIAM DE PAOR

shall not have died in vain—that this nation, under God, shall have
a new birth of freedom—and that government of the people, by
the people, for the people, shall not perish from the earth.[41]

Pearse in his peroration said:

Our foes are strong and wise and wary; but, strong and wise and
wary as they are, they cannot undo the miracles of God who ripens
in the hearts of young men the seeds sown by the young men of a
former generation. And the seeds sown by the young men of '65
and '67 are coming to their miraculous ripening today. Rulers and
Defenders of Realms had need to be wary if they would guard
against such processes. Life springs from death; and from the graves
of patriot men and women spring living nations. The Defenders of
this Realm have worked well in secret and in the open. They think
that they have purchased half of us and intimidated the other half.
They think that they have foreseen everything, have provided
against everything; but the fools! the fools! the fools!: they have left
us our Fenian dead; and while Ireland holds these graves, Ireland
unfree shall never be at peace.[42]

Now, in 1916, it is revealed that while the defenders of the realm were
working in secret and in the open, so were their enemies. Earlier, in 1913,
Pearse had said at Tone's grave:

We have come to the holiest place in Ireland, holier to us even
than the place where Patrick sleeps in Down. Patrick brought us
life, but this man died for us.

But now, in the inversion of the Proclamation, the emphasis is on the
living, not the dead. The trumpet has sounded. Ireland has trained her
manhood 'through her secret revolutionary organisation, the Irish
Republican Brotherhood, and through her open military organisations ...'
There is a triumphalist note. The Volunteers, parading with their inadequate weapons, or none, and in their makeshift uniforms, or none, had
been figures of fun to many in the populace for the past year or so, in a
world filled with the deadly figures of real soldiers. Now, it is proclaimed,
they too have become real soldiers, and it is *Ireland* that has now put an

army into the field and is, as it emerges, a belligerent in her own right in the Great War.

This is a defiance founded on a political tradition, shared (as many of Ireland's political traditions were and are) by Orange and Green. The right of citizens to bear arms was incorporated in the Bill of Rights passed by the English Parliament in October, 1689, in consequence of the 'Glorious Revolution' of 1688, which, dethroning James II in favour of his son-in-law William of Orange and his daughter Mary, curbed the absolute power of the monarchy. Like the American Declaration of Independence nearly a century later, the Declaration of Rights (which gave rise to the Bill), had begun by listing grievances against the deposed king. Then it went on to establish rights independent of the king's prerogative. The Bill included the clauses:

> That the raising or keeping of a standing army within the kingdom in time of peace, unless it be with the consent of parliament, is against law.
>
> That the subjects which are Protestants, may have arms of their defence suitable to their conditions, and as allowed by law.[43]

The Americans, after their Revolution, adopted their Constitution in 1788, but shortly afterwards, in 1791, added ten amendments which constitute the American Bill of Rights. Amendment 2 (whose meaning is still vigorously debated in the United States) reads:

> A well-regulated militia being necessary to the security of a free state, the right of the people to keep and bear arms shall not be infringed.

It was in this spirit, if not on this principle, that the formation of companies of Volunteers, electing their own officers (as distinct fom a militia under martial law), began, initially in Belfast in August 1778, to defend the country against the French at a time when the regular British forces on this side of the Atlantic were inadequate. The Volunteers of 1778 set a precedent, and the principle of the right to bear arms was remembered by nationalists. Thomas Davis referred to the Volunteers in restating the principle:

To carry arms is the first right of man, for arms are the guardians of property, honour, and life. God gave weapons, as well as clothing, to the lion and the eagle; but to man he gave skill to furnish himself with all bodily comforts, and with weapons to defend them, and all his other rights, against every assailant, be he the beast of the forest or the tyrant of society.

To carry arms is the ultimate guarantee of life, property and freedom. To be without the power of resisting oppression is to be a slave ... Arms and liberty are synonymous.[44]

Pearse had the same view and expressed it forcefully in November 1913, in respect of the foundation of the Ulster Volunteer Force at the end of 1912 (announced in January 1913):

It is symptomatic of the attitude of the Irish Nationalist that when he ridicules the Orangeman he ridicules him not for his numerous foolish beliefs, but for his readiness to fight in defence of those beliefs. But this is exactly wrong. The Orangeman is ridiculous in so far as he believes incredible things; he is estimable in so far as he is willing and able to fight in defence of what he believes. It is foolish of an Orangeman to believe that his personal liberty is threatened by Home Rule; but, granting that he believes that, it is not only in the highest degree common sense, but it is his clear duty to arm in defence of his threatened liberty. Personally, I think the Orangeman with a rifle a much less ridiculous figure than the Nationalist without a rifle ...[45]

Ireland has 'patiently perfected her discipline'. Again, this is an inversion and a rebuttal: the Volunteers and the Citizen Army, it asserts, had not been children at play, or mountebanks on a stage: they had followed a hard and deadly course. Yeats, in his great poem on the Rising, was to say that he (like so many) had been:

... certain that they and I
But lived where motley is worn ...

but then—

All changed, changed utterly:
A terrible beauty is born.[46]

They had waited for the day. '*Der Tag*': the concept was familiar enough at the beginning of the Great War:

Now God be thanked who has matched us with His Hour,
And caught our youth, and wakened us from sleeping ...[47]

It had long been a cherished imagining within the Fenian tradition; not merely a question of England's difficulty being Ireland's opportunity—as the old saying had it—but simply the idea that in the fulness of time the hour would strike, the day would dawn, when it would be right and opportune to rise again. 'Fáinne Geal an Lae'—'The Bright Dawning of the Day'—was a song the insurgents sang in the Post Office.

Within the Fenian tradition, in Ireland, but even more in America, the day's dawn had been long awaited, and the postponement of action (even at the most inopportune moments) had frequently been cursed. These words about organization, discipline, and the right moment are addressed, not so much to 'the people of Ireland' as to the initiates of the movement. In particular, perhaps, they are addressed to the impatient Americans of Clan na Gael. Taking action at last, action represented as the end of disciplined and sustained planning and endeavour—'seizing the moment'—would, among other things, open American purses and enlist American agitators, propagandists and organizers in the cause of the newly proclaimed republic.

### ... and, supported by her exiled children in America ...

Support from America was more important than this brief reference would suggest; but the Proclamation strives above all to declare that Ireland is acting autonomously as a sovereign nation in making war. America had to be acknowledged but is here represented, as it were, as an extension of Ireland. It is still Ireland's 'children' who provide the support.

It is very doubtful if radical separatist nationalism could have maintained itself in Ireland into the twentieth century had it not been for the great migrations of the nineteenth century, which brought millions of Irish people overseas, many of them to Britain, Australia, Canada and elsewhere, but extraordinary numbers, after the famine of the 1840s in particular, to the United States. To call them 'exiled children' is to say that they had been banished; and this indeed is how nationalists saw the history of the migrations: Irish people had been driven out of their country by British government, or misgovernment. And that is how the emigrants and their children and their children's children saw it. (They failed, of course, to foresee the continued emigration under native Irish governments.)

Further, in America (to take just that large and most significant segment of the migration) they found freedom, not just freedom from the rule of another country or an alien queen or king, but freedom from the deferential and subservient sub-feudal society of Victorian and Edwardian British polity, with its sycophantic hierarchies in their malign Irish manifestations. In America, in the later nineteenth century, they found democracy. The men who came back (usually only to visit their homeland) stood up straight and could look a policeman in the eye. And by the late nineteenth century, the intransigent opponents of any British rule in Ireland, if they were a minority within the country (which, in the absence of a plebiscite, is far from certain), could probably be counted as part of a majority of Irish opinion, taking the post-Famine migrants and their children overseas into account. America, then and in the early twentieth century, was, for them, the foster parent of the Irish Republic.

At the same time, the people in America who gave direct and material as well as moral support to the organization of the rising, although many of them may have been born in Ireland, were not Irish but Irish-American: their lives and futures and the future of their posterity were committed in and to the New World. They tended to be impatient with the hesitancies and tergiversations of those in Ireland who aimed at separation from England but who, being still ensnared in the web of Old World history, had to adjust all the time to the circumstances of a society in which the enemies of their purpose could claim privilege and enjoy an arrogant power. These Irish-Americans demanded radical action. And their help was essential, if only because it was in neutral America that it was possible to conduct the initial negotiations with the Germans to make feasible the alliance that would give credibility to a declaration of war against England. Several of the signatories of the Proclamation had direct experience of America. They all knew that Clan na Gael was an ally as indispensable as imperial Germany. They all knew also that the reference to Irish-American support was a threat. The United States was neutral in the war, and a strong popular sentiment was in favour of remaining neutral. It was a presidential election year, and this was to be an issue: President Wilson would campaign for re-election on his success in keeping America out of the war, although he was already strongly inclined to the British cause. The policy of the British government, on the other hand, was to do all possible to bring the United States in as an ally (it was already becoming clear that this was essential for Allied success). The Rising, with its appeal to a large body of opinion in America, could well endanger this policy. Were the Rising, simultaneous in Dublin, Cork, Galway, Sligo and Limerick, to force on the British a sustained effort at reconquest, with consequent great bloodshed, world opinion, including much American opinion, could well be affronted. Certainly the British propaganda which represented the war as having been engaged for the defence of small nations would be, in part at least, undone.

### ... and by gallant Allies in Europe, ...

There is a lapse here into the cant phraseology of the Great War. 'Gallant' is a word whose usage for the past year and a half had been in the propaganda bulletins of the belligerents. With its connotation of chivalrous or courteous behavior it also has a suggestion of a brave but forlorn hope. 'Gallant little Belgium' had suffered the German onslaught in 1914 and had been regularly offered as a cause in the endeavour to recruit Irishmen (although for this purpose it had as commonly been described as 'Catholic Belgium'). The small British Expeditionary Force that fought at Mons had been 'gallant'. The word belongs to that '"raised", essentially feudal language' of the time, discussed by Paul Fussell. In his glossary, or 'table of equivalents', he gives it: 'To be earnestly brave is to be *gallant*.'[48] It may be employed here with some intention of irony, since it is applied, not to those to whom British newspapers and propagandists had made it exclusive, but to 'the Hun'. However, it may be that irony was not intended. Pearse was receptive to the 'high diction' of the war, and Connolly seemed recently to have come round to it. Plunkett, who had dealt with the Germans, was given to romantic language, and may have suggested this insert.

For the 'gallant allies in Europe' were the Germans. The Austrians and the Turks hardly entered the picture. It was the German empire that had conducted most of the anti-Allied propaganda in America and had endeavoured to build up German-American agitation, to prevent American help for the Allied side in the War and, as far as possible, to support the war efforts of the Central Powers. It was the German empire's Foreign Office and other such imperial agencies—in particular the admiralty—who felt there might be some advantage to their cause in providing help to the Clan na Gael and IRB purpose of insurrection against the British government in Ireland. Immediately on the outbreak of the war, Devoy of Clan na Gael, acting at the behest of the IRB, had approached Count von Bernstorff, the German Ambassador in Washington, with the request for help. Bernstorff transmitted the request to Berlin. He himself had some doubts on the matter: he was anxious not to antagonize unduly the Anglophile American establishment, to which he was socially and personally attracted, since it was a much more powerful and influential group then than the American-Irish interest, and he had doubts about the determination and capacity of the Irish would-be insurgents. There seems also to have been some reluctance among the rulers of Germany, an imperial power, to aid rebels against another imperial power, not to speak of the German army's contempt for 'civilian soldiers' and hatred of *francs-tireurs*; but this, in wartime, was a scruple not too difficult to put aside. Maintaining American neutrality was in Germany's interest; as was the making of peace again with England (which seemed possible and desirable in the early stage of the war); but so, of course, was defeating England. The Germans looked into the matter.

It happened that Sir Roger Casement, not a member of the IRB, but a friend of MacNeill and Hobson, had sailed for America at the beginning of July 1914, with an introduction from Hobson to Devoy, to raise money for the newly formed Volunteers, of which he was one of the founders. Just before leaving Ireland, he had attended that meeting of the Provisional Committee of the Volunteers which acceded to Redmond's demand for twenty-five places. Casement, with Hobson, had voted to admit Redmond's nominees (although very reluctantly). Because of this vote, Devoy—briefed by Clarke, who regarded it as treachery—at first treated him with great suspicion, but on the outbreak of the war, having made contact with Bernstorff, and after consultation with his Clan colleague Joe McGarrity, he thought the gentlemanly Casement, a former diplomat, might be persuasive with the Germans. Casement, with Devoy's approval, composed the address that was transmitted to the kaiser, asking the Germans to make peace by 'effecting the independence of Ireland, and securing its recognition as a fixed condition of final settlement between the great maritime powers'.[49] Casement's personal sympathies, apart from his passionate patriotism, lay fervently with the Germans, whom (especially from his experiences in southern Africa) he greatly admired, and even loved. In this he differed from most of the Clan na Gael, IRB and Volunteer leaders, who saw in Germany, in the war, merely a means to the end they desired. In September, he sent a letter to the *Irish Independent*, arguing that Ireland should not be involved in the war on England's side. This made it virtually impossible for him (a pensioner of the British Consular Service) to return to Ireland. Instead, he persuaded Bernstorff and the military attaché in Washington, Franz von Papen, that he should go to Germany to negotiate and to try to persuade Irishmen in the British army who had been captured in the early German advances to change sides and be trained for an expedition to fight the British in Ireland. This was agreed, and, financed by Clan na Gael, he sailed for Germany by way of Norway, and arrived in Berlin on 31 October. His efforts at recruiting an Irish Brigade from the prisoners of war were ultimately unsuccessful. Meantime the IRB's military council gathered detailed intelligence on the British order of battle in Ireland, to be supplied to Berlin, and continued their efforts to arrange an arms shipment. Joseph Plunkett travelled to Germany by a roundabout way through France, Spain, Italy and Switzerland and arrived in Berlin on the morning of 20 April 1915.[50] He joined with Casement and negotiated with the German Chancellor, Bethmann Hollweg, for the landing of arms in Ireland in the spring of 1916. The details were worked out in the course of the following year.

In the event, the German government—at the behest of the Irish conspirators—sent its supply ship, with 20,000 rifles and four machine guns, but without radio, to the south-west coast of Ireland. The arms were to be landed at Fenit, and the ship, the *Libau*, formerly the British (Wilson Line) merchant ship *Castro*, from Hull, which had been taken as a prize by the German Navy early in the war, now masquerading as the Norwegian ship *Aud*, arrived in Tralee Bay on the evening of Holy Thursday. When the ship was at sea, the Volunteers tried to postpone its arrival by a crucial day or so but were unable to communicate this. The ship was taken by the British navy, but was scuttled by her crew. Casement (with two others) landed from a U-boat on Banna Strand near Fenit early on Good Friday, hoping to prevent the rising, and was shortly afterwards arrested.[51]

The German alliance had been regarded without enthusiasm by the IRB, but it was essential to their original plans. British anti-German propaganda at the beginning of the war was extremely mendacious, and was discounted; but the truth (as reported, for example, by neutral American war correspondents) about the Germans' brutality and barbarism in their march through Belgium was sufficiently repulsive. All the group who signed the Proclamation, however, had counted on the arms shipment. While the guns were being landed and distributed in the west of Ireland, there was to be a German naval demonstration off the east coast of England to distract the British and in particular to divert some of their naval force. We can imagine that, had the arms arrived safely and been distributed safely, had the original plan been about to be applied, the phrase about 'gallant allies' in the Proclamation might have been somewhat longer, somewhat more positive and somewhat more explicit: imperial Germany would have been more plainly acknowledged as an ally. As it was, this partly veiled reference was sufficient to cover the possibility that Germany, even now, might find means to take advantage of the opportunity for its cause provided by the Rising.

### ... but relying first on her own strength ...

The vision of most of the insurgent leaders derived from a sacred, sustaining and magisterial story, or myth, the story of Ireland as the narrative of a quest for freedom. It is a narrative as conventional as a fairytale, as powerfully marked by motifs which offer a guide through a moral maze. Betrayal is a recurring theme; the ruin of endeavour by spies and informers. This lesson the planners of the Rising learned: they kept their counsel and chose their confidants well. There were no informers in 1916. Another recurring theme was the folly of relying on foreign help—an important consideration in view of the emphasis both in Irish literary tradition and in folklore on the prospect of redemption coming from overseas. One of the songs of the insurgents contrived to combine the notion of help from abroad with the affirmation of self-reliance:

> Tá Gráinne Mhaol ag teacht thar sáile,
> Fianna Fáil ina mbuíonn gárda,
> Gaeil féin a's ní Franncaigh ná Spáinnigh,
> A's ruaigeart ar na Gallaibh.

[Granuaile is coming over the sea,
Ireland's troops forming the vanguard,
Gaels themselves, neither French nor Spaniards,
To the routing of the foreigners.]

### *... she strikes in full confidence of victory.*

Irony. Had the rising begun as planned, the writers of the Proclamation might have had *some* prospect, in the context of the Great War, of a victory of sorts. As it was, on Easter Monday they had begun a militarily hopeless endeavour. The 'full confidence of victory' may carry over from the draft prepared before all the preparations went wrong. (It was also a standard expression in the war communiqués announcing offensives and the like, as when the Russian Grand Duke Nicholas, about to lead his ill-prepared army into battle on 14 August 1914, telegraphed to Joffre in France that 'firm in the conviction of victory' he would move against the Germans.) But it must be recognised too that an element of self-delusion was necessary to the Provisional Government's enterprise (and was already being displayed). It was an ingredient of the courage and confidence they showed in the face of mundane and bleak reality. It was necessary too, to sustain the morale of the insurgent soldiers and auxiliaries and to seek to persuade the Irish people to whom the Proclamation was addressed. 'Full confidence of victory' was both fantasy and propaganda.

## 4. THE THIRD PARAGRAPH

### *We declare the right of the people of Ireland to the ownership of Ireland, and to the unfettered control of Irish destinies, to be sovereign and indefeasible.*

There is a change of mode here. The declaration of war has been made. Now a paragraph begins setting forth the principle on which the declaration is founded, the right which is being asserted in arms. This is the equivalent of the 'self-evident truths' of the American Declaration of Independence; the affirmation of fundamental political principles. But it is not an affirmation either of the social contract or of Tom Paine's 'Rights of Man'; rather, something more and something slightly different. The 'right' asserted is not that of individuals, but of a collective, 'the people of

Ireland'. It compares more closely with Clause IV of the French Declaration of the Rights of Man and of the Citizen:

> The Nation is essentially the source of all sovereignty; nor can any individual, or any body of men, be entitled to any authority which is not expressly derived from it.

The American Declaration speaks of 'unalienable' rights (of 'all men'), that is, rights which cannot be transferred to another. The French Declaration lists rights that are 'natural, imprescriptible and inalienable' (in Tom Paine's contemporary translation), that is, rights ('of man') which are founded in nature and can neither lapse through the passage of time nor be transferred. The Proclamation is not initially concerned with such 'rights', but with a 'right' (of the people of Ireland), which is supreme and cannot be annulled ('sovereign and indefeasible'); overriding therefore, it could be inferred, such rights as 'life, liberty and the pursuit of happiness'. But such an inference would be mistaken; for this passage in the Proclamation is but a condensation of Pearse's final pamphlet, *The Sovereign People* (31 March 1916), which he prefaced with the words, 'For my part, I have no more to say.' He summarized his views on national sovereignty in 'a few simple propositions':

1. The end of freedom is human happiness.
2. The end of national freedom is individual freedom; therefore, individual happiness.
3. National freedom implies national sovereignty.
4. National sovereignty implies control of all the moral and material resources of the nation.

He went on:

> Now, the good of the nation means ultimately the good of the individual men and women who compose the nation. Physically considered, what does a nation consist of? It consists of its men and women, without any exceptions ... The right and privilege to make laws or to administer laws does not reside in any class within the nation; it resides in the whole nation, that is, in the whole people, and can be lawfully exercised only by those to whom it is delegated

by the whole people. The right to the control of the material resources of the nation does not reside in any individual or in any class of individuals; it resides in the whole people, and in the manner in which the whole people ordains. Once more, no individual right is good as against the right of the whole people; but the people, in exercising its sovereign rights, is morally bound to consider individual rights, to do equity between itself and each of the individuals that compose it as well as to see that equity is done between individual and individual.[52]

He makes it clear that in large part this formulation is based on the writings of Wolfe Tone. In particular he refers to a secret manifesto issued to the Friends of Freedom in Ireland in June 1791, 'attributed to Tone in collaboration with Neilson and others', from which he quotes with particular approval the passage:

The inherent and indefeasible claims of every free nation to rest in this nation—the will and the power to be happy, to pursue the common weal as an individual pursues his private welfare, and to stand in insulated independence, an imperatorial people.

And he goes on:

The deep and radical nature of Tone's revolutionary work, the subtlety and power of the man himself, cannot be grasped unless it is clearly remembered that this is the secret manifesto of the movement of which the carefully constitutional declaration of the United Irishmen is the public manifesto.[53]

There is some uncertainty on the question of property. Pearse had gone on to write:

To insist upon the sovereign control of the nation over all the property within the nation is not to disallow the right to private property. It is for the nation to determine to what extent private property may be held by its members, and in what items of the nation's material resources private property may be allowed.[54]

The nation is sovereign—although the word 'people' is preferred here in the Proclamation. The 'right' so claimed for it is twofold, and in this there are hints of an ambiguity, or at least a dichotomy, that runs through the document. It is a right, firstly, to 'the ownership of Ireland', and in this expression, stronger than the 'sovereign control' of Pearse's pamphlet, there is almost certainly buried a compromise between the views of the Citizen Army and the views of many of the Volunteers. 'The people' are (or 'is'?) entitled to 'the *ownership* of Ireland'. What does this mean? The hand of Connolly may be discerned here. He had given one answer, earlier in the year:

> All the material of distribution—the railways, the canals, and all the land stolen from the Irish people in the past, and not since restored in some manner to the actual tillers of the soil, ought at once to be confiscated and made the property of the Irish *State* ... all the factories and workshops owned by people who do not yield allegiance to an Irish Government immediately on its proclamation should at once be confiscated and their productive powers applied to the service of the community loyal to Ireland, and to the army at its service.[55]

And again (modifying his position slightly after coming to his agreement with the IRB and the Volunteers):

> Recognising that the proper utilisation of the national resources requires control of political power, we propose to conquer that political power through a working-class political party; and recognising that the full development of national power requires complete national freedom, we are frankly and unreservedly prepared for whatever struggle may be necessary to conquer for Ireland her place among the nations of the earth.[56]

The second element of the 'right' claimed for the people of Ireland is 'the unfettered control of Irish destinies'. This is a reiteration of the right of national sovereignty and is an affirmation of extreme separatism, since it implies an absolute parting with the British empire. It goes far beyond what was intended in Home Rule. 'Going beyond', indeed is inappropriate: it is a concept wholly different from Home Rule. Europe was, of course, at war in 1916, but it was still a continent of empires headed by emperors or monarchs, the British, the Russian, the French, the German, the Austro-Hungarian, the Spanish, the Belgian, the Dutch and the Turkish, all or most of which governed suppressed, and sometimes oppressed, nationalities at home and overseas. Home Rule was intended to be no more than a modification of that pattern. A British liberal paper wrote on the election of John Redmond to the leadership of the reunited Irish Party in 1900 (reactivating Home Rule as an issue in British politics) that:

> Ireland has proved herself a sub-nationality within the Empire. The French Canadians may or may not be such a community, the Cape Dutch may or may not be, but the Irish most undoubtedly are. With such a policy there are two ways of dealing. You may occupy militarily and govern despotically, or you may grant local self-government: there is no other way.[57]

The 'right' here asserted was to reject this system completely. It was the third way.

***The long usurpation of that right by a foreign people and government has not extinguished the right, nor can it ever be extinguished except by the destruction of the Irish people.***

The Proclamation here turns to history, and the history is the heroic myth that had been adumbrated by Pearse, particularly in his more recent writings. That myth, like all such sacred drama, embodied a truth: that the configuration of the recent centuries of Irish history had set a large part of the Irish people—conquered and long rejected in their own country—in opposition to those who ruled over them and in resentment at their deprivation. Those who ruled over them, proximately, were the dispossessors, the 'Protestant Ascendancy', as they had come to be known; but nationalism for two centuries and more had taught that the true object of resentment and hostility should be the power that maintained that ascendancy: England. And nationalism had projected the antagonism back for further centuries into the past, so that the many-sided and complex conflicts of twelfth- and thirteenth-century Ireland were simplified into a war between Ireland and England. This simplified story had taken shape in the bitter context of seventeenth-century religious and ideological war and had given rise to an historiography which asserted itself against the contrary, self-serving, historiography of the conquest, the establishment historiography, venerating its own myth—a version of what Kipling had called 'the White Man's burden'.

For Pearse, separatism was the theme of seven centuries of Irish history before his time:

> It will be conceded to me that the Irish who opposed the landing of the English in 1169 were Separatists. Else why oppose those who came to annex? It will be conceded that the twelve generations of the Irish nation, the 'mere Irish' of the English state-papers, who maintained a winning fight against English domination in Ireland from 1169 to 1509 (roughly speaking), were Separatist generations.[58]

This is to transpose, inappropriately, twentieth-century political concepts into the very different world of the twelfth century. What is most inappropriate is the idea of 'Separatists'. (Besides: those who first opposed the landing in 1169 of the Cambro-Norman-led Welsh and Flemish men-at-arms who were mercenary allies of the Irish king of Leinster were the Norse of Waterford.) Yet, the myth, the sacred narrative, still embodies a truth: the collapse of Ireland's barely achieved political unity at the time of the Norman settlement, the establishment of the English monarchs' Lordship of Ireland, equivocally acknowledged by the Irish provincial kings, and episodic conflict between the rulers of England and native rulers in Ireland over several centuries, leading to the Tudor and Stuart conquest. The 'long usurpation of that right by a foreign people', therefore, extends back, in this concept, for more than seven hundred years. And the word 'foreign' has a political, a separatist, force. 'Gall' in early medieval Ireland meant just that—foreign, non-Irish—and was contrasted with 'Gael'—native. Later in the Middle Ages and in early modern Ireland, 'Gall' often meant one of settler descent, as distinct from a 'Gael', one of native descent, both being 'Éireannaigh'—Irish. There were in this sense many 'Gaill' in the Ireland of 1916. But modern separatism—rejection of the English in all their pretensions in Ireland—required an emphasis that would sharply divide the 'British Isles' (a term in itself hateful to nationalists): they were 'a foreign people'.

The 'usurpation' of the 'right' refers, essentially, to the English claim to possess Ireland by right of conquest, which right is here categorically denied. It is a claim buried under the temporizings of nineteenth-century politics, but still the rock bottom of England's argument for ruling Ireland, when it came down to legal and constitutional argument (insofar as it could come to such debate under an administration founded upon the same claim). The eighteenth century, nearer to the event of conquest, had, sometimes, a clearer mind on the subject than had the nineteenth. Dr Smollett, in the third volume of his *Present State of All Nations*, wrote:

> Setting aside the ridiculous legends and fables of the Irish with respect to their antiquity and origin, it seems highly reasonable to conclude, that the country was first peopled from Britain. There is no good reason to induce us to believe that it was ever conquered by the Romans. Towards the decline of the Roman empire, a colony of Scots began to make a great figure in Ireland, whence it acquired the name of Scotia. The island was afterwards often har-rassed by the Danes, Norwegians and Saxons; but never entirely subdued, till Henry II, King of England, made himself master of it in the twelfth century. It has been ever since subject to the kings of England, who were only styled lords of Ireland, till the title of king was bestowed on Henry VIII, in 1541, by the states of the realm in Parliament assembled.[59]

The case was more bluntly, and less erroneously, stated more than once in the late eighteenth century, when the 'patriot' party or faction in the Irish House of Commons debated painfully how they might achieve an accommodation with the numerous Catholics in the cause of Irish independence and at the same time—deprived by their independence of the support of Great Britain—maintain their own position in the country. The realists (or the cynical) who opposed them pointed out that what they held in Ireland was not theirs by any natural right of the social contract kind, but by right of conquest. This was a right of mere force; and they must hold on, or lose. Their argument anticipated the 'What we have we hold' of later unionist Ulster. So, for example, Mr Dennis Browne, rep-resenting Trinity College, Dublin, in the Irish House of Commons, spoke there on 20 February 1787 in support of Government (in a debate on a Government measure—described by opposition speakers as draconian—to put down disturbances in some southern counties, connected with refusal to pay tithe) and agreed with a recent pamphlet:

That there was a faction in the country (and so there was, and no man could deny it) hostile to the established church, hostile to the protestant ascendancy, hostile to the acts of settlement, and the titles to their estates. That the property of the country differed from that of any other country in the world. In other countries the landed title is purchase, here it is forfeiture. The old proprietor feeds the eternal memory of his ancient claim. The property of this country resembles the thin soil of volcanic countries, lightly spread over subterraneous fires.

And later, speaking in support of the proposed Act of Union, Fitzgibbon, Lord Clare, similarly said:

The whole power and property of the country has been conferred by successive monarchs of England upon an English colony composed of three sets of English adventurers who have poured into this country at the termination of three successive rebellions—confiscation is their common title; and from their first confiscation they have been hemmed in, on every side, by the old inhabitants of the island, brooding over their discontent in sullen indignation.

These emphasize what was near to the hearts of the speakers, landed property, but the same argument had application in the matter of politics—'the power and property of the country'—and the discontent of 'the old inhabitants' referred to by Fitzgibbon had survived, indeed grown, throughout the nineteenth century as a reversionary interest. It rejected what a resolution of the United Irishmen of Dublin in 1792 had called:

... in the governing portion of the people a habit of domination. This *Habit*, mixing with the antipathies of past times, and the irritations of the moment, has impressed a strange persuasion, that the rights of the plurality are *Protestant* property, and that the birth-right of millions, born and to be born, continue the spoils of war and booty of conquest.[60]

In rejecting 'the long usurpation of that right', the Proclamation here threatened, on behalf of the dispossessed, the dispossessors with dispossession.

So far as landed property was concerned that reversal was already in progress, not necessarily to the advantage of the intentions of the Proclamation. For the land was already passing into the hands, not of 'the people of Ireland', but of the tenant farmers, not restoring an old land-holding system, but creating a new proprietorship, which would inevitably be tenaciously conservative of the transfer. In more general terms, the political threat by the dispossessed to those who now possessed, was a threat to reverse history. But history is 'the arrow of time', which flies from the bow to the mark, but can't be persuaded to spring back from the target to the slackened string. The authors of the Proclamation were clearly thinking here as separatists and addressing their rejection of the 'usurpation' to England; but the usurpation had created layers and levels of vested interest, not necessarily of property, within Ireland, interests which had an independent, now Irish, existence. The authors go on, in the next paragraph of the Proclamation, to attempt to address those interests, but by proclaiming the undoing of history, they mire themselves in an unavoidable contradiction.

**In every generation the Irish people have asserted their right to national freedom and sovereignty: six times during the past three hundred years they have asserted it in arms.**

Here again, Pearse condenses some of his recent writings and appeals more directly to history. He was concerned about the generations: it was a long time since 1867 (the abortive Fenian uprising). It was necessary for his schematic myth that there *should* be a rising in each generation; but something had gone wrong in the previous twenty or thirty years:

> There has been nothing more terrible in Irish history than the failure of the last generation. Other generations have failed in Ireland, but they have failed nobly; or, failing ignobly, some man among them has redeemed them from infamy by the splendour of his protest. But the failure of the last generation has been mean and shameful, and no man has arisen from it to say or do a splendid thing in virtue of which it shall be forgiven.[61]

So he wrote late in 1915. Now he counts, in this statement in the Proclamation, six 'assertions in arms' in three hundred years—since 1616.

These are most probably the episodes of 1641, 1689, 1798, 1803, 1848 and 1867. If so, it is a very stylized and rhetorical history. The wars that began in Ireland in 1641 and 1689 could be described as dynastic and civil wars; they could also be described, in their Irish aspects in particular, as religious wars, Catholic against Protestant. That 'the Irish people' in them 'asserted their right to national freedom' is, however, at best debatable; the Confederate Catholics at Kilkenny had put forward the case that Ireland was a distinct and separate kingdom under the Stuart crown; but that is not quite the same thing. The case could certainly be put that it happened in 1798. The uprisings of that year were both popular and widespread, and the republican leaders proclaimed national independence. And, while Emmet's uprising of 1803 was limited and local in the event, it had a measure of popular support, and undoubtedly was to be endorsed throughout the nineteenth century in the memory of a large part of the people. The episodes of 1848 and 1867 can at best be described as aborted uprisings; not assertions of their right in arms by 'the Irish people', although many had sympathy for the would-be insurrectionists and their aims.

But this poetic history, supplemented by the statement of republican ideology, is the essence of the Proclamation. It is a mythic definition of Ireland, powerful because it is transcendental, raising its vision above the shameful contingencies of the present, to find a future in the transfigured past.

*Standing on that fundamental right and again asserting it in arms in the face of the world, we hereby proclaim the Irish Republic as a Sovereign Independent State, and we pledge our lives and the lives of our comrades-in-arms to the cause of its freedom, of its welfare, and of its exaltation among the nations.*

The formal proclamation. It may be based, loosely, on that final paragraph of the American Declaration of Independence in which the independence of the colonies is formally stated. But there are significant differences. The authors of the Declaration wrote that

> We ... declare That these United Colonies are, and of Right ought to be Free and Independent States; that they are absolved from all Allegiance to the British Crown ...

No such absolution was sought or granted by the authors of the Proclamation, who are announcing (in their own voice, and presumably in their capacity as the now-established Provisional Government) not that the Republic should be or was about to be, but that it *is*.

The pledge immediately following the formal Proclamation is probably suggested by the American document; but the difference is both subtle and profound. The American text of the relevant passage, already quoted earlier in full, reads:

> And for the support of this Declaration, with a firm reliance on the Protection of Divine Providence, we mutually pledge to each other our Lives, our Fortunes and our sacred Honor.

This was a *mutual* pledge of total commitment under God: a covenant, in the sense in which that concept had become established in Protestant thought—referring back to the many covenants of the Old Testament:

> And God spake unto Noah, and to his sons with him, saying, And I, behold, I establish my covenant with you, and with your seed after you ...[62]

It had acquired a special meaning in Scotland, but also in sixteenth- and seventeenth-century England and in colonial America. William Haller writes of the early Puritan sects:

> The inner organization of the sect was necessarily democratic. Its strength depended directly upon the number of those who freely consented to the authority of the group and its leader ... Two notable devices serving to this end ... were early resorted to. The first was the covenant, a solemn pledge, a contract, entered into by the members with one another and with God, to adhere to the congregation and never to depart ...[63]

The minds of the Founding Fathers, deists and Freemasons though they largely were, were cast in the mould of the Protestant Reformation, including in its products Puritan New England and the Presbyterian and Quaker Middle Colonies. The authors of the Proclamation had minds of a different mould; and if they were following the American founders in entering their pledge immediately after the formal declaration of independence, it was a different pledge. It was a simple soldiers' commitment of their lives to the newly proclaimed republic, and to its 'exaltation among the nations'. They were pledging not merely to be 'prepared for whatever struggle may be necessary to conquer for Ireland her place among the nations of the earth', as Connolly had put it (echoing Emmet), but to aim at something more: Ireland was not just to take her place but to have a high place; to be 'exalted'.

## 5. THE FOURTH PARAGRAPH

**The Irish Republic is entitled to, and hereby claims, the allegiance of every Irishman and Irishwoman.**

The voice has changed again. The previous paragraph was spoken by the members of the Provisional Government: 'We declare ...' Now we are back in the third person, but—the interesting moral and intellectual logic of the Proclamation being followed meticulously—it is now, no longer 'Ireland', but the newly proclaimed 'Irish Republic', who is speaking, claiming, after that proclamation, the allegiance of *every* Irishman and Irishwoman.

For the whole of this short fourth paragraph of the Proclamation is addressed to a problem which was insoluble, taking into account the aspirations of the signatories within the circumstances of the time. It is addressed to the secession—from the Home Rule cause and perhaps from Ireland—of the unionists of Ulster.

But this first sentence, although that is its purport, is much more general in its terms—demanding the allegiance of '*every* Irishman and Irishwoman'. It is a bold demand indeed, in 1916, but the only one that could possibly be made in the circumstances with any semblance of credibility. It implies a question: 'Whose side are you on?' And it suggests very clearly that, after generations of fudging, in this time of crisis a choice, simple and binding, had to be made. It demanded the equivalent of a leap of faith: '*Credo quia absurdam*'; or, to put it in more extreme form:

> So then because thou art lukewarm, and neither cold nor hot, I will spew thee out of my mouth.[64]

In a sense this single sentence sums up what the Proclamation was issued for: to call on the people of Ireland to make up their minds finally to be free. It has to be read in the context of the earlier paragraphs: *Ireland*, now assuming the garb of the Republic, has the authority to command her children.

Although this command is issued to all her children, it is addressed particularly—as the remainder of the paragraph makes clear—to those in the north who were (foolishly and mistakenly in the view of the Proclamation) renouncing their allegiance to Ireland.

*The Republic guarantees religious and civil liberty, equal rights and equal opportunities to all its citizens, and declares its resolve to pursue the happiness and prosperity of the whole nation and of all its parts, cherishing all the children of the nation equally, and oblivious of the differences carefully fostered by an alien government, which have divided a minority from the majority in the past.*

This is a response to another portentous document of the time—the 'Ulster Covenant', to which more than 200,000 people had subscribed on 28 September 1912, and tens of thousands thereafter:

> Being convinced in our consciences that Home Rule would be disastrous to the material well-being of Ulster as well as to the whole of Ireland, subversive of our civil and *religious freedom*, destructive of our citizenship, and perilous to the unity of the Empire, we, whose names are underwritten, men of Ulster, loyal subjects of His Gracious Majesty King George v, humbly relying on the God whom our fathers in days of stress and trial confidently trusted, do hereby pledge ourselves in solemn Covenant throughout this time of threatened calamity to stand by one another in defending for ourselves and our children our cherished position of equal citizenship in the United Kingdom, and in using all means which may be found necessary to defeat the present conspiracy to set up a Home Rule parliament in Ireland ...[65]

(The italics have been added here to indicate the point at which the Covenant is echoed by the Proclamation.)

By 1916, partition of the country, in the form of a proposed amendment to the Government of Ireland Act 1914 (the suspended Home Rule

Act), had already been conceded in principle by the British Government to Craig and Carson. The signatories of the Proclamation had no substantive response to what had become the secession of Ulster unionism from the Irish unity that had subsisted under the British crown, and largely under British government, for the previous two hundred years. Engaging in what by now must seem already a forlorn endeavour to free Ireland from British rule, dedicated by their principles (both the republican and the socialist principles) to the equal treatment of all Irish people as citizens, constrained in their fight by paucity of means, they could only state their principles in respect of the Ulster Protestants and make, for the record, an appeal which they knew must fall on deaf ears but which they hoped would be heard in the future. Just before the outbreak of the Great War there had been much talk of civil war within the United Kingdom on the Irish—the Ulster—question. Superficially, it had seemed for a while in 1914 as if the forces of the crown might be engaged against the Ulster Volunteer Force to enforce a Home Rule Act; but this was a superficial appearance: the British establishment had a natural sympathy with the Ulster resistance to Home Rule, and king, army and opposition were lining up against the Government (which had Ulster sympathisers in its own ranks) when the outbreak of the Great War intervened. Although Home Rule was by then passing into law, its operation was suspended, and straightaway bargaining was resumed to secure a separate arrangement in Ulster: partition. The bargain had in effect been struck. All this had happened by Easter, 1916.

In the circumstances, the best that the Proclamation could do was to emphasize that the republican principles of liberty, equality and fraternity, which are recited in this paragraph, would apply not only to nationalists, not only to the 'Gael', not only to Catholic Ireland, but to all:

> ... *religious and civil liberty*, equal rights and equal opportunities to all its citizens ... to pursue the happiness and prosperity of the *whole* nation and of *all* its parts, cherishing all the children of the nation equally, *and oblivious of the differences carefully fostered by an alien government, which have divided a minority from the majority in the past.* [Emphasis added.]

(The phrase 'cherishing all the children of the nation equally' has been frequently misread to refer specifically to children. Both both from its context here and from the repeated usage in the Proclamation, it is plain that 'all the children of the nation' meant 'all the people of Ireland'.) The offered guarantees reflect not only a republican but, again, a socialist, or near socialist, thinking ('equal opportunities' in 1916 came from that side of the political debate). The promise to be 'oblivious of the differences' was one that could hardly be fulfilled—both Pearse and Connolly were only too aware of the differences and had shown it in their writings. What they intended, or rather wished for, was that the differences would disappear; the Proclamation calls again upon history, to suggest that these differences were externally inspired and that, with independence, they would fade away. The implied accusation is that English government had caused the Ulster opposition to Home Rule by a calculated policy of '*Divide et impera*'. There is, of course, truth in this, to the extent that British politicians, in and out of government, who opposed Home Rule for Ireland, had been prepared to 'play the Orange card', against those other politicians who were in favour of Home Rule. But, as the signatories of the Proclamation well knew, some of them from direct personal experience, this was only because the 'Orange card' was already there to play.

Their long-term aspiration plainly was to persuade their Ulster opponents that they were Irish, owed an allegiance to Ireland, and would benefit from throwing their lot in with Ireland rather than with England. The signatories could have had no illusion about their chances of achieving this persuasion simply by the fourth paragraph of the Proclamation. That was for the future. But the paragraph had to go into such an epochal document.

And there had been some portents to suggest that ultimate persuasion was not wholly impossible. When the IRB was reorganizing ten or fifteen years earlier, it had been especially active in Ulster and the Ulster borderlands. There were Protestant nationalists in some numbers then in Ulster, some of them republicans. The Independent Orange Order of the time seemed to be reaching out to nationalist opinion. One of the difficulties the separatists encountered was the hostility, not of Protestant Orangemen but of Catholic nationalists (especially along the borders of Ulster) to republican ecumenism. Bulmer Hobson (a Belfast Quaker), for example, electioneering in Leitrim, met the opposition of Catholic clergy in the border counties and of the Catholic bigotry of the Ancient Order of Hibernians.[66]

More recently, a few days after the landing of arms for the UVF at Larne on 24 April 1914, there had been a hint of conciliation from unionism. Carson, a Dublin man, who had hoped to hold all Ireland in the

Union and was not anxious for partition, responding to a suggestion by Winston Churchill in the House of Commons, had said:

> If Home Rule is to pass, much as I detest it, and little as I will take the responsibility for the passing of it, my earnest hope, and indeed I would say my earnest prayer would be that the Government of Ireland for the South and West would prove and might prove such a success in the future, notwithstanding all our anticipations, that it might even be for the interests of Ulster itself to move toward that Government, and come in under it and form one unit in relation to Ireland. May I say something more than that? I would be glad to see such a state of things arising in Ireland in which you would find the mutual confidence and goodwill between all classes in Ireland as would lead to a stronger Ireland in a federal scheme.[67]

But Redmond had not responded to Carson's subsequent tentative approach to an accommodation. There was, therefore, some very slight reason for nationalists to persuade themselves that the Ulster unionists could ultimately be persuaded; but, as Brian Inglis has pointed out, it was unrealistic. Carson's offer of 1914, he explains, lacked force:

> But Carson was no longer in control. His value to Craig had been his influence at Westminster; now, Westminster mattered less to Craig. The Curragh and Larne had left his position so strong that Carson was almost expendable. Personally, Craig might have accepted Carson's and Ervine's view. A united Ireland dominated by Ulster would be an attractive proposition. But he would hardly be able to put it across to the Covenanters, conditioned as they had been to believe that they would be at the mercy of the Catholic majority in the South.[68]

And the offer was not resumed. Earlier than that, at the time of the foundation of the Ulster Volunteer Force, Pearse had optimistically written:

> One great source of misunderstanding has now disappeared: it has become clear within the last few years that the Orangeman is no more loyal to England than we are. He wants the Union because he imagines that it secures his prosperity; but he is ready to fire on

the Union flag the moment it threatens his prosperity. The position is perfectly plain and understandable. Foolish notions of loyalty to England being eliminated, it is a matter for business-like negotiation. A Nationalist mission to North-East Ulster would possibly effect some good. The case might be put thus: Hitherto England has governed Ireland through the Orange Lodges; she now proposes to govern Ireland through the A.O.H. You object: so do we. Why not unite and get rid of the English? They are the real difficulty; their presence here the real incongruity.[69]

Those wishful thoughts of 1913, of course, distorted the meaning of what had happened and was happening in the North. It is true that Ulster unionists thought that Home Rule would place their prosperity in jeopardy. But there was a great deal more to their opposition that that. Their own mythic history was very different from that which Pearse and other nationalists had been expounding. They saw themselves—those who were the counterparts to the nationalists in their thinking—as a people of exodus. Ireland was not the ancient motherland of their ancestors; it was the land their forefathers had won, as the Dutch had won South Africa, as others of their forefathers had won the American frontier. The evidence for their outlook was abundantly available. But, not only the authors of the Proclamation, but nationalists much less radical in their views, felt constrained to see Ulster unionism as an aberration, or as a disease that could be cured. On the ground, in Ulster, there were many who saw it otherwise, who saw Protestant Ulster as a foe to be defeated, much as Pearse and his colleagues saw England as a foe to be defeated. This 'Hibernian' outlook was opposed by republicans; but they could neither extirpate it nor come to terms with the reality of demotic—as distinct from ascendancy and functionary—unionism.

No nationalist, of any stripe, could have been optimistic about Ulster at Easter, 1916. Civil war in Ireland had barely been averted or postponed, by the outbreak of the Great War; nothing had been solved. But hope was always possible, and the paragraph of the Proclamation addressed to the Ulster problem must be regarded as springing from hope—as well as being a statement of goodwill and honest intention. But the paradox of the republic is like the paradox of the Irish tricolour: its ecumenical intent was seen as its greatest threat.

## 6. THE FIFTH PARAGRAPH

*Until our arms have brought the opportune moment for the establishment of a permanent National Government, representative of the whole people of Ireland and elected by the suffrages of all her men and women, the Provisional Government, hereby constituted, will administer the civil and military affairs of the Republic in trust for the people.*

There is no reason to believe that this statement is not truthful and sincere; but inevitably, in the strange circumstances, it is the statement of a junta executing a coup. 'Hereby constituted' begs some questions. According to Ruth Dudley Edwards:

> The revolutionaries had made some small provision for the day of victory, however unlikely. A provisional government, less abhorrent to the people than they were, had been selected—Alderman Tom Kelly, Arthur Griffith, William O'Brien, Mrs Sheehy-Skeffington and Seán T. O'Kelly (Sinn Féin, Sinn Féin, Labour, Suffragette-socialist and Sinn Féin respectively). It is most unlikely that any of these prominent citizens knew of the august role for which they had been chosen—except O'Kelly, who was secretly a member of the IRB, and was to suffer some anguish after his arrest lest the British authorities should have discovered his 'importance'; in case Tom Kelly refused the chair, Seán T. was to direct the civil government.[70]

What is clear enough is that what the insurgents envisaged for the republic which they had just proclaimed was a system of representative government, with universal—including female—adult suffrage. Women's suffrage, still after much agitation not granted in the British system, was of course one of the major political issues of the days just before the outbreak of the war. Like so much else, the resolution of the question and been postponed in United Kingdom politics until after the war which was now in progress. But it is here plainly declared as part of the policy of the new Irish Republic.

## 7. THE SIXTH PARAGRAPH

***We place the cause of the Irish Republic under the protection of the Most
High God, Whose blessing we invoke upon our arms ...***

The Great War had been in progress for a year and a half. At its beginning, the weight of informed opinion had been that it couldn't last much
more than six weeks or so—it was widely believed (partly because of the
influence of Norman Angell's book of 1910, *The Great Illusion*) that
modern war would be so costly that the powers could not sustain it for
much longer. Now there was no end in sight—costly both in lives and in
goods although the war had indeed proven to be. April 1916 was about
the last moment in which the other illusions of 1914 could still persist.
The terrible battle (if battle be the word for such prolonged warfare) of
Verdun had begun with the German offensive on the Western Front on
21 February, and for more than a month now this had settled into a war
of attrition. The casualties had been very high in 1914 in the early mobile
warfare; they had been high at Gallipoli in 1915 in the major, unsuccessful, British attempt to avoid the deadlocked confrontation of the Western
Front and turn the flank of the Central Powers. The great British army of
volunteers called into being by Kitchener (which included the Ulster
Division and the tens of thousands of other Irishmen who had joined up
since late 1914) was being deployed for action in France, but had not yet
been committed to 'the mincing machine', as the French and Germans
already had. It was still, just, possible without revulsion or irony to call
down God's blessing on arms—as had been done since the days of
medieval chivalry.

For the last paragraph of the Proclamation reverts to the 'high diction'
discussed by Fussell and already referred to. Blessings had been called
down all over Europe in 1914, on guns, on bayonets, on swords and banners. Many had blessed the war itself. As late as December 1915, Pearse
had described 'the last sixteen months' as 'the most glorious in the history
of Europe'. He had gone on to say that:

> War is a terrible thing, but war is not an evil thing. It is the things
> that make war necessary that are evil. The tyrannies that wars break,
> the lying formulae that wars overthrow, the hypocrisies that wars
> strip naked, are evil. Many people in Ireland dread war because

they do not know it. Ireland has not known the exhilaration of war for over a hundred years. Yet who will say that she has known the blessings of peace? When war comes to Ireland, she must welcome it as she would welcome the Angel of God.[71]

He has been somewhat unfairly singled out for blame for this passage, as if his opinion were quite eccentric: it was, on the contrary, in the early days of the war, commonplace in its outlook. To take the single example of Austria, Hermann Bahr, who had spoken at the Stockholm peace conference of 1910, became a militarist in 1914, writing in his *Kriegssegen*, that 'we, insofar as there are Germans in this wide, wide world, all bless, bless, bless this war!' The most unwarlike Rainer Maria Rilke, during the early days of the war, wrote his *Fünf Gesänge*, summoning the God of battle. Musil and Hofmannstahl wrote high-toned patriotic essays in support of the war effort. The atheist Freud, if he did not ask for God's blessing, invoked his own gods and wrote in 1914 that 'All my libido is given to Austria-Hungary.' God is summoned into the very weapons themselves in their killing work in the words of the worker-poet Alfons Petzold, written in 1914:

> O, dass ich könnte jetzt in jeder Kugel sein,
> die frölich zischend ein rotes Menschenherz grüsst!
> O, dass ich könnte jetzt atmen mit jeder Säbelklinge,
> die flammenrash ein weises Menschenhirn küst!
> So in ein ganz fremdes Leben eintauchen,
> als zerstörende Kraft, aus der Neues entblüht—
> wäre das nicht eine Freude, die sonnst in Gott nur glüht?

> [Oh that now I might be in each bullet
> That hisses joyfully to greet a red human heart!
> Oh that I might breathe with every sabre blade
> That, flame-swift, kisses a sage human brain!
> To be transmuted to such strange new life
> When might, destroying, once again deflowers—
> Would not this be supreme good fortune,
> Such shining joy as otherwise is God's alone?]

The leader for many years of the Austrian peace movement, Peter Rosegger, wrote during the war:

O Herrgott, schütz mein deutsches Volk
In seiner Ehr und stolzen Kraft ...
Beschütze, Gott, mein Österreich ...
O grosser Herrgott, lass uns siegen![72]

[O Lord God, guard my German people
In proud and honourable might ...
Safeguard, God, my Austria ...
O grant us, great Lord God, to win!][73]

And in the other European nations there were similar, almost identical outpourings. God was appealed to to bless every cause, to bless the swords, the banners, the cannon—not specially, however, the machine guns or the barbed wire or the mustard gas. The favoured collective name for them was 'the sword'. But all causes were just: there was a competition for God. The solemn prayer which opens this last paragraph of the Proclamation echoes the prayers that had gone up from Vienna, Berlin, Belgrade, St Petersburg, Paris, Brussels and London.

*... and we pray that no one who serves that cause will dishonour it by cowardice, inhumanity, or rapine.*

The army of the Irish Republic was made up neither of conscripts nor of mercenaries but of unpaid volunteers. It is appealed to here to behave in a way not usual with armies; but, again, this is the 'high diction' of the time. It is the sort of appeal that had been made to the 'Kitchener army', of paid volunteers, recruited to the British service since shortly after the outbreak of the war and now mustering on the Western Front. It is part of the spirit of the time—as well as being in the tradition taught in the schools of Irish nationalism—that the civilian soldiers, of whom there were millions now in Europe, should be 'worthy' of whatever high cause they were defending. Outside Russia and the Balkans, war was virtually unknown to the European generation of 1914. The powers had been at peace with one another since 1871 and war was approached through veils of illusion woven by boys' literature of the turn of the century, by the art of academic 'history' painters, and by the new popular press that had come into being in the past thirty years or so. Personified nations—as in the cartoons of *Punch*—wielded 'swords of light' and led dedicated acolytes to apotheosis in the high destinies of their nations. The 'age of the masses' had arrived, and this was the pabulum of the masses, forked out as provender for them by the 'mass media' (not yet so named, but already in existence). The chivalrous medieval knight was a 'pre-Raphaelite' image of the age. 'Rapine' had been part of the stock-in-trade of real medieval knights, as had inhumanity (robbing and killing people, and not just their knightly enemies, was their prerogative), nor were they forbidden to modern regular armies. The country houses of the United Kingdom, for example, were well furnished by 1916 with Chinese trophies, the spoils brought home from the looting of the Summer Palace in the suppression of the 'Boxer Rebellion' of 1900—the fruits of 'rapine'. But war, which for centuries had been well understood for what it was by merchants and peasants—and, indeed, by its practitioners—was in the early twentieth century, presented—'packaged' as we might now say—to the ploughmen and clerks, the artisans and gentlemen's sons, the millworkers and domestic servants of the early twentieth century as a practice of high idealism.

The knightly ideal held up to the army of the Irish Republic was that which had been enunciated by Pearse in an address to Na Fianna Éireann in February 1914:

> ... when Patrick asked Caoilte Mac Rónáin how it came that the Fianna won all their battles, Caoilte replied: 'Strength that was in our hands, truth that was on our lips, and purity that was in our hearts'.[74]

It was not only the pledged combatants who were called to this ideal, but all who 'served that cause'—and all had been called to this service.

*In this supreme hour the Irish nation must, by its valour and discipline and by the readiness of its children to sacrifice themselves for the common good, prove itself worthy of the august destiny to which it is called.*

With perfect symmetry the Proclamation concludes as it had begun: '... Ireland ... summons her children to her flag ...' The 'Irish nation' has now, in the final sentence, become, or been equated with, the people, its children. It is commanded (by the Provisional Government which, in two or three paragraphs, has become assured in its authority) to sacrifice for 'the common good', and 'to prove itself worthy'. There is here a clear, and dangerous, suggestion of a sovereign nation, to which the people who constitute that nation must be subordinate.

What is the 'august destiny' of which it must prove itself worthy? Freedom, independence, obviously. But more is implied. August or high destinies were in fashion at the time of the beginning of the Great War. Russia (the future 'Third Rome'); Austria (in spite of Napoleon, the Holy Empire still, the divinely ordained governor of Christendom); France (the Republic, the liberator and light of the world); England (the ocean-ruling arbiter of the commercial and moral affairs of humankind); Germany (the bearer of culture, of thought, of science, of discipline); America (the city set upon a hill, the 'last, best hope of humankind'): all freely acknowledged their destiny, chosen by God for an imperial greatness that would justify the human race. Ireland's destiny, we can infer—not from the Proclamation, which is silent on the subject, but from the thoughts, expressed elsewhere, which lay behind it—was to be once again in the future, as she was held to have been in the past, the teacher of Europe— perhaps now of the world—the bearer of Christian truth and ancient wisdom; the most ancient of the European nations, as she would be the most enduring:

> When the life of the cities of Europe goes
> The way of Memphis and Babylon,
> In Ireland still the mystic rose
> Will shine as it of old has shone.[75]

### THE SIGNATORIES

*Signed on behalf of the Provisional Government,*
*Thomas J. Clarke, Seán Mac Diarmada, Thomas MacDonagh,*
*P.H. Pearse, Éamonn Ceannt, James Connolly, Joseph Plunkett.*

The signatories of the Proclamation were ordinary, some of them obscure, men, who had however the comparatively rare gift of making something of their lives, addressing themselves to a transcendental purpose, rather than accepting the world as they found it and scraping out a living, or hacking and cajoling a career, each for himself. They were those whom Yeats had met:

... Coming with vivid faces
From counter or desk among grey
Eighteenth-century houses.

Clarke was fifty-nine years old, a singleminded and embittered man, born in England to Irish parents who took him to South Africa before returning to Co. Tyrone when he was ten; he went to America at the age of twenty-one and joined Clan na Gael, was arrested on a mission to London in 1883, at the time of the London dynamite campaign and condemned to penal servitude for life; released after fifteen years he returned to America and then, in 1907, returned to Dublin and resumed or continued his revolutionary plotting, using as bases his two newspaper shops in the city centre. Mac Diarmada, a Co. Leitrim man, was thirty-two; a fluent speaker of Irish, a member of the Gaelic League since 1902 and of the IRB since 1906, a charmer of women, a diligent organizer and dedicated revolutionary, afflicted with a limp since he suffered from poliomyelitis in 1912; he was, with Clarke, one of the chief planners of the Rising. MacDonagh was thirty-eight, a native of Co. Tipperary who had come to Dublin in 1908 to help Pearse found his school, St Enda's; teaching since 1912 in University College, Dublin, he was a poet, familiar with European literature in several languages, fluent in Irish, sociable and pleasant-mannered and at home in a literary salon; he was Director of Training of the Volunteers. Pearse was thirty-seven, born in Dublin, the son of an English stonecarver whose main business was making tombstones and of an Irish mother; a failure at law (which he reckoned a virtue); active successfully since his youth in the affairs of the Gaelic League, and editor of its paper *An Claidheamh Soluis*; an educational theorist and reformer and founder of Scoil Éanna (St Enda's School); one of the founders and chief organizers of the Volunteers; a compelling orator who was awkward or aloof in private company; a poet and polemicist, careless of everyday business affairs but singleminded and effective in the undertakings that engaged his serious attention. Ceannt was forty-two, active in the Gaelic League, a traditional musician and a member of the Pipers' Club; active in the organization of the Volunteers from their foundation. Connolly was forty-eight, born in Edinburgh of Irish parents, a British soldier as a boy, who deserted in Ireland; he returned to Dublin again in 1896, where he founded the Irish Socialist Republican Party; he later founded the Irish Labour Party; he spent seven years in the United

States, where he was active in the Industrial Workers of the World; he then organized the Transport Workers' Union in Belfast, was in Dublin for the 1913 lock-out, and was founder of the Irish Citizen Army; largely self-taught, he was a theorist and forceful socialist writer. Plunkett was twenty-nine, born in Dublin, the son of Count Plunkett; tubercular and sickly since childhood, he lived and travelled abroad for his health but became active in cultural activities, founding the *Irish Review* with his friend Thomas MacDonagh, who was teaching him Irish, and the Irish Theatre with Edward Martyn; he too was a poet.

When they signed the Proclamation they must have been reasonably certain that in consequence they would soon be dead. That in itself entitles the document to some serious consideration. But they could not have foreseen even that death with certainty, and they could have foreseen nothing else of the course of events to come; not even the shape of the Rising which they were about to begin. As I write these words, at the beginning of August 1996, more than eighty years have gone by since they were shot by firing squads. We have the advantage of those eighty years of hindsight; but understanding of the Proclamation will benefit from leaving aside for the moment all knowledge of what was to come, and trying to hear it as it was read aloud, fresh from the printers, outside the General Post Office in Dublin at about 12.45 p.m. on Easter Monday, 24 April 1916. The Rising was unexpected by the multitude. Pearse stepping out of the Post Office to read the Proclamation was like Moses going 'down from the mount unto the people'—coming from without a cloud. The Proclamation has a religious tone to it: it is a call to repentance; a call to the people to be worthy of their 'august destiny'. If we look beyond its words to read what those who composed or endorsed them had been writing and saying elsewhere, especially in private communications, we find a common emotion: a compound of rage, despair and disgust at the shoddiness and pettiness of early twentieth-century Ireland. It is expressed not only by separatist nationalists but also by a variety of writers, including Yeats, Joyce, Shaw and Stephens. A new beginning is proclaimed on Easter Monday, a rebirth, a resurrection.

But the Ireland who addresses the people in the Proclamation is a Janus, looking back through the mists of time to a vanished glory; looking forward to the rights of woman and man in the twentieth century. There is in this the potential for deep division or for a dynamic tension generating energy.

There are, in the final analysis, only two political parties in the Western world: those who take sides with the weak and the poor, and those who take sides with the rich and the powerful. The signatories of the Proclamation had a clear position on this ultimate issue. It was summed up by Pearse two and a half years earlier:

> God knows that we, poor remnant of a gallant nation, endure enough shame in common to make us brothers. And yet here is a matter in which I cannot rest neutral. My instinct is with the land-less man against the lord of lands, and with the breadless man against the master of millions. I may be wrong, but I do hold it a most terrible sin that there should be landless men in this island of waste yet fertile valleys, and that here should be breadless men in this city where great fortunes are made and enjoyed.[76]

Cutting across this fundamental social and political opposition, there is another: between the deep human need for community, which is expressed in nationalism, in religion, in language and custom, and the modern universalist liberal concept of *individual* freedom and of the 'rights' of all men (and women) to 'life, liberty and the pursuit of happiness'. To reconcile these, which the signatories attempted, is to undertake the res-olution of a contradiction; but the contradiction still shows through their skilful words, as it does throughout the history of the modern Western world.

# Afterword: Liam de Paor, 1926–98

## MICHAEL RYAN

Liam always told a romantic story about how his parents met. His father came from Tramore to Dublin on Easter Monday 1916 to interview for a railway job but when he arrived, things were not quite as he had expected. He had to find temporary lodgings near Kingsbridge (Heuston) Station because getting around the city was impossible with the unexpected outbreak of warfare. He stayed in a nearby house owned by the Burke family. Liam's mother was a daughter of the house and worked as a VAD nurse. On the Tuesday of Easter Week she set out for her duties having to pass by an army barricade en route. Liam often said that she thought then for the first time that she was 'on the wrong side'. His father, Paul Power, and Kathleen Burke hit it off and eventually married. Liam was born in Dublin on 13 April 1926. He went to the local National School in Drumcondra and received his secondary education at Coláiste Mhuire. Winning a scholarship to university, he began to study architecture at University College, Dublin, but abandoned his studies in 1945 to work for a time as a cartoonist at the Harry Clarke Stained Glass Studios.

In 1950, he got a job as an architectural assistant in the National Monuments Branch of the Office of Public Works and rapidly became involved in the survey and conservation of national monuments and in particular of the ancient buildings of Skellig Michael and the Cistercian Abbey of Mellifont in Co. Louth. He had to keep both tasks running concurrently, which was a stretch. His survey of the monastery of Skellig was the influential modern account until recent work began on the site. His Mellifont tasks included excavation and supervision of the partial reconstruction of architectural features—the Lavabo or wash house was one of his achievements. In those days responsibility was devolved far down the scale and de Paor was exceptionally alert to seize every opportunity to do excellent and, for the time, ground-breaking work. Nobody then or since had quite his professional formation—archaeological and basic architectural training and draughtsmanship—not many in immediately post-war Ireland could match his education and expertise. He seems at the time to have been very consciously an intellectual, reading widely and as he once told me, keeping a record in his diary of the books he was reading—it was something that had a flavour of the great Enlightenment and the nineteenth-century thinkers.

Devoted to archaeology, he completed a bachelor's degree in Celtic Studies in his spare time and submitted a thesis for the award of a masters' on Romanesque architecture in Ireland for which he was awarded a travelling studentship by the National University. He spent a couple of years abroad reading and observing, especially in Germany. He missed nothing of any use or interest with his keen eye, remarkably clear vision and accurate recording of places and things and his rummaging in museum collections for unconsidered trifles. Not all was serious of course, and he claimed that during a prolonged stay in Munich his fellow students often passed him off to strangers in bars as an Eskimo—given the flatish planes of his face and dark eyes, it was a good a ploy as any to break the ice and hoover up some free beers.

He taught archaeology at University College, Dublin, in the later fifties where he met Máire McDermott also an archaeologist and his future wife. Together they wrote *Early Christian Ireland*, for its time, a surprisingly clear-headed, deeply learned and enjoyable book, which is still valuable. He served briefly as Executive Secretary of the Royal Irish Academy and spent a year with UNESCO in Nepal advising on the conservation of cultural properties. On his return from Nepal he was appointed to a lectureship in history at UCD where he taught until his retirement in 1986. For a distinguished medievalist he is best remembered by many for his deeply researched and emotionally empathetic essays on modern Irish history and Ireland's place in Europe and for his timely, wise and honourable *Divided Ulster*. Politically he was a Labour supporter and understood deeply the need to hear the other side in the Irish argument. When I first encountered him in the mid-1960s he was a doubly welcome lecturer on early Ireland who managed to combine the history and archaeology of Ireland with those of Europe—years later when I followed some of the paths he opened for us I realised just what a fine and prescient scholar he was. Once in a review the tribute that 'he was incapable of writing a boring sentence' was paid to him. As a conversationalist he was witty and penetrating and as an acute observer of the cultural and political scenes his recollections and anecdotes were both illuminating and sometimes startling. One of these sticks in my mind and it concerns a weekend organised by a community of priests in Dublin at the very beginning of the armed campaigns in Northern Ireland in 1970; a handful of intellectuals and politically knowledgeable people were brought together with an equal number of 'activists' and paired off for a weekend of conversations. Liam's roommate was a well-known abstentionist 'parliamentarian' who took no interest in debate or any 'other side' and who boasted for two days without a break that the spell had been broken and that a young man had been induced to kill and so his movement had been blooded and from then on things would be easier. Liam masked his disgust in the interests of dialogue but that was something he never forgot. On another occasion at Amherst, MA, he spoke of the shared history of the Irish North and South at the Battle of the Somme only to be told afterwards by a future prominent UDA figure that his was a good talk and that he agreed with his historical account but that the Somme was 'their' legend and not his.

It is as a writer that de Paor is best remembered and his clear, elegant style enabled him to write effectively for the specialist as well as the wider audiences. No publication of his was ever dull, ever lacking in insight, or above all, ever without decency and humanity. Why he was never appointed to a position of influence in his chosen fields is hard to understand. That neither he nor Máire continued to work in archaeology in UCD after the death of their mentor, the distinguished Seán P. Ó Ríordáin, to help build on that professor's visionary approach to archaeology, seems to have been a diversion from an obvious and decisive path. UCD later gave him a different home—in history—where arguably he had the freedom to be the public intellectual politically engaged, elegantly trained as he was. He became a superb communicator, remarkably for someone who appeared diffident and shy on many occasions.

The last decade and a half of his life were extremely productive, marked by the appearance of *St Patrick's World* and collections of essays such as *Ireland and Early Europe*. His examination of the Proclamation of 1916, which we celebrate here, was published in 1997 and is, if anything, more necessary to read now than at any time in the almost twenty years that have passed since it appeared. He left hospital to be present at the launch of his final book a few weeks before his death in 1998. Entitled *Landscapes with Figures* it is a collection of essays of characteristic brilliance. After his retirement from University College, Dublin, he obtained support from the government to work on the publication of his major excavations at Inis Cealtra, Lough Derg, Co. Clare, and at Tihilly, Co. Offaly, and Ardagh, Co. Longford. He was making steady progress on these and on an autobiography, sadly unfinished, at the time of his death in 1998. I had the privilege of reading the chapters as he drafted them.

I remember Liam first as an approachable and conscientious teacher in UCD in the mid-1960s, and later as a distinguished elder scholar, generally pleasant and open but a keen and respectful disputant when challenged. In the late 1970s, I spent some time with him in Boston and later in Germany. When I worked in Shewsbury Road in the 1990s he became a regular visitor and lunch companion and once we went on a prolonged expedition together to Galway to a conference and thence to Derry for what we now know was NOT the 1,300th anniversary of St Colmcille's death. He filled the long hours of driving and the occasional dull patches in the celebrations with anecdotes, pithy mini-lectures on places we passed, political commentary and a restrained geniality towards the world and its odder inhabitants. He was however incensed at a colleague's poor grasp, and reading of, an Old Irish poem. A rarefied aesthetic. I was just getting to know him properly when his final illness struck and even then his curiosity and penchant for research didn't desert him—in the one brief conversation we had in hospital about his illness, I left feeling hopeful and interested and almost reassured.

# Notes

Material in square brackets has been added by the editor.

1 [On Tuesday 21 January 1919, the members of Dáil Éireann heard a 'Democratic Programme' read into their proceedings: it opened with an explicit
acknowledgment of the 1916 Proclamation.]

2 See Julian P. Boyd, *The Declaration of Independence: the Evolution of the Text as
Shown in Facsimiles of Various Drafts by its Author, Thomas Jefferson* (Princeton:
Princeton University Press, 1945). Also, Garry Wills, *Inventing America:
Jefferson's Declaration of Independence* (New York: Doubleday, 1978).

3 Anon. (i.e., by James Wilson), *Considerations on the Nature and Extent of the
Legislative Authority of the British Parliament* (Philadelphia: at the London
Coffee-house, 1774). See Wills, *Inventing America*, pp 248, 250, 251.

4 Wills, *Inventing America*, pp 240 ff.

5 Joseph Lortz, *The Reformation in Germany* (trans. Ronald Walls) (London,
New York: Herder and Herder, 1968), p. 346.

6 For the text see Merryn Williams (ed.), *Revolutions, 1775–1830* (London:
Penguin in Association with the Open University, 1971), pp 99ff where it is
quoted from Tom Paine, *The Rights of Man* (1791), Part One.

7 Karl Barth, *Protestant Thought: From Rousseau to Rischl* (New York: Harper,
1959), p. 28.

8 Quoted by J.F. Bosher, *The French Revolution* (New York, London: Norton,
1988), p. 148, in an interesting passage on the liberalism of Louis XVI.

9 [Published texts of Irish House of Commons performances varied consider-
ably even in newspapers of the day. Subsequent 'polishing' was also common.
For a synthetic edition of Grattan, see his posthumous *Miscellaneous Works*
(London: Longman etc.; Dublin: Milliken, 1822).]

10 Plato, *The Republic*. Para 501a. [Cf. Plato, *Complete Works* (ed. John M.
Cooper) (Indianapolis: Hackett, 1997), p. 1122.]

11 Tom Garvin, *Nationalist Revolutionaries in Ireland, 1858–1928* (Oxford:
Clarendon Press, 1987), p. 14.

12 [For Parnell's speech on 21 January 1885, from which this paragraph is taken,
see a longer extract in the *Cork Examiner*, 22 January 1885, varying in minor
detail.]

13 John Redmond, 'Introduction' to Michael MacDonagh, *The Irish at the Front*
(London: Hodder & Stoughton, 1916).

14 See Séamus Ó Buachalla (ed.), *The Letters of P.H. Pearse* (Gerrards Cross: Smythe, 1980), p. 362.

15 See Ruth Dudley Edwards, *Patrick Pearse: the Triumph of Failure* (London: Gollancz, 1977), pp 264–74.

16 For an account of this important gathering, see Proinsias Mac Aoghusa, *Ar Son na Gaeilge: Conradh na Gaeilge, 1893–1993; Stair Sheanchais* (Baile Atha Cliath: Conradh na Gaeilge, 1993), pp 146–50.

17 P.H. Pearse, 'The Coming Revolution' in *Political Writings and Speeches* (Dublin, Cork: Phoenix, 1924), p. 94.

18 For the Gaelic text, see P.H. Pearse, *Scríbhinní* (Baile Atha Cliath: Phoenix, 1924), pp 266–7.

19 Pearse, 'How Does She Stand?' in *Political Writings*, p. 63.

20 For further discussion, see in particular Tom Paine, *The Rights of Man* (1791/2) Part Two (London: Penguin, 1969), pp 200ff. Also R.R. Palmer, *The Age of the Democratic Revolution: a Political History of Europe and America 1760–1800* (Princeton: Princeton University Press, 1959), vol. 1 (*The Challenge*), pp 13–20.

21 Thomas Jones, *Whitehall Diary*, vol. 3 (ed. Keith Middlemass) (London: Oxford University Press, 1971), p. 89.

22 The major European powers, having set up a separate Belgian state, imposed Leopold of Saxe-Coburg as king in 1831, to whom they also offered the crown of Greece, where they were setting up an independent state at the same time. Leopold declined the Greek gift, which was then offered in 1832 to Otto, second son of the king of Bavaria, who accepted.

23 The members of the Provisional Government of Ulster were the duke of Abercorn; H.T. Barrie MP; R. Dawson Bates; Sir Edward Carson KC, MP (presiding); James Chambers KC, MP; C.C. Craig MP; Captain James Craig MP; John Gordon KC, MP; A.L. Horner KC, MP; Peter Kerr-Smiley MP; Sir John Lonsdale Bt, MP; Col. J.L. McCalmont MP; W.J.M. McCaw MP; R.J. McMordie MP, lord mayor of Belfast; Ronald MacNeill MP; William Moore MP; Captain the Hon. Arthur O'Neill MP; William Moore MP; George Sclater [sic recte]; Col. R.G. Sharman-Crawford MP; Rt. Hon. Thomas Sinclair PC; Col. Robert Wallace, Grandmaster of the Orange Order.

24 Helen Landreth, *The Pursuit of Robert Emmet* (New York, 1948), p. 191.

25 John O'Leary, *Recollections of Fenians and Fenianism* (London: Downey, 1896), p. 119.

26 'Address to the Volunteers of Ireland, Issued from the Society of United Irishmen of Dublin, 14th December 1792' (William Drennan in the chair, Archibald Hamilton Rowan, secretary). *Proceedings of the Society of United Irishmen of Dublin* (Philadelphia: Jacob Johnson, 1795).

27 W.W. Seward, *Collectanea Politica*, vol. 1 (Dublin: Wogan, 1801), p. 30.

28 An unsuccessful political party of the 1940s, led by Gearóid Ó Cuinneagáin, had plans for a capital city on the Hill of Tara. [See R.M. Douglas, *Architects of the Resurrection: Ailtirí na hAiséirghe and the Fascist 'New Order' in Ireland* (Manchester: Manchester University Press, 2009).]

29 Terence Mac Swiney, *Principles of Freedom* (Dublin: Talbot Press, 1921) (re-issued Port Washington, NY; London: Kennikat Press, 1970), pp 135–7.

30 Women were not admitted to membership of the Orange Order.

31 Thucydides, *The Peloponnesian War* (ed. J.H. Finley; trans. Richard Crawley) (New York: Random House, 1951), p. 103.

32 Abraham Lincoln, *Speeches and Writings* (ed. Don E. Fehrenbacher) (New York: Library of America, 1989), vol. 2, p. 103.

33 Aristophanes, *Three Comedies* (ed. William Arrowsmith) (Ann Arbor: University of Michigan Press, 1969), p. 50.

34 G.A. Hayes-McCoy, *A History of Irish Flags* (Dublin: Academy Press, 1979), p. 204.

35 See Thomas Pakenham, *The Year of Liberty: the Story of the Great Irish Rebellion of 1798* (London: Hodder & Stoughton, 1969), plate facing p. 128.

36 A 'contemporary account' quoted by Desmond Ryan in 'Stephens, Devoy and Tom Clarke', *University Review*, vol. 1, no. 12 (1957), p. 47.

37 George Sigerson, *The Last Independent Parliament of Ireland: with Account of the Survival of the Nation and its Lifework* (Dublin: Gill, 1918), p. 19.

38 Speaking on 23 September 1912 at a great anti-Home-Rule rally at Craigavon; see A.T.Q. Stewart, *The Ulster Crisis: Resistance to Home Rule 1912–1914* (London: Faber, 1967), pp 47–8.

39 James Stephens, *The Insurrection in Dublin* (Dublin: Maunsel, 1916), p. 66.

40 For discussion, see Garry Wills, *Lincoln at Gettysburg: the Words that Remade America* (New York: Simon & Schuster, 1992).

41 There are several variations in records of this famous speech; see Don E. Fehrenbacher's edition of Lincoln, *Speeches and Writings* already cited.

42 Pearse, 'O'Donovan Rossa: Graveside Panegyric', *Political Writings*, pp 136–7.

43 See Gerard M. Straka (ed.), *The Revolution of 1688 and the Birth of the English Nation*, 2nd ed. (Lexington, MA: D.C. Heath, 1973), p. 65.

44 Arthur Griffith (ed.), *Thomas Davis: the Thinker and Teacher: the Essence of His Writings in Prose and Poetry* (Dublin: M.H. Gill, 1914), pp 67–8.

45 Pearse, 'From a Hermitage', *Political Writings*, p. 185.

46 W.B. Yeats, 'Easter 1916', *The Poems* (ed. Daniel Albright) (London: Everyman's Library, 1992), pp 228–30.

47 Rupert Brooke, 'Peace' in *Collected Poems* (New York: John Lane, 1915), p. 107. [For some pertinent comments, see Robert Wohl, *The Generation of 1914* (Cambridge, MA: Harvard University Press, 1980), pp 85–95. Dealing with

Spanish literary intellectuals of this period, Wohl (p. 125) uses the term 'regenerationism', which in some respects meets the Pearsean requirements. However, Pearse was less keen to supersede his preceding generation than (somehow) to take its place, to *become* it and thus redeem it. This regressive urge did not go unnoticed at the time: see J.M. Synge, 'Can We Go Back into Our Mother's Womb?' (1907), *Collected Works, Vol. II: Prose* (ed. Alan Price) (London: Oxford University Press, 1966), pp 399–400.]

48 Paul Fussell, *The Great War and Modern Memory* (London: Oxford University Press, 1975) pp 21–2.

49 On these initial negotiations, see Brian Inglis, *Roger Casement* (London: Hodder and Stoughton, 1974), pp 275–86.

50 Plunkett's diary of this journey is published in *University Review*, vol. 1, no. 11 (1957), 32–48.

51 For a concise account of these events, see Florence O'Donoghue's foreword to Karl Spindler, *The Mystery of the Casement Ship* (Tralee: Anvil, 1965).

52 Pearse, 'The Sovereign People', *Political Writings*, pp 337–8.

53 Pearse, 'The Separatist Idea', *Political Writings*, p. 276.

54 Pearse, 'The Sovereign People', *Political Writings*, p. 339.

55 James Connolly, in *The Workers' Republic*, 15 January 1916.

56 Connolly, *The Workers' Republic*, 29 January 1916.

57 *The Speaker*, 10 February 1900; quoted in L.G. Redmond-Howard, *John Redmond: the Man and the Demand*, 2nd ed. (London: Everett, 1912), p. 101.

58 Pearse, 'Ghosts' (December 1915), *Political Writings*, pp 232–3.

59 [Richard Twiss], *A Tour of Ireland in 1775* (London: for the author, 1777), p. 151.

60 From 'Address to the Friends of the People at London, Issuing from the Society of United Irishmen of Dublin, 26th October 1792'. *Proceedings of the Society of United Irishmen of Dublin* (Philadelphia: Johnson, 1795).

61 Pearse, 'Ghosts', *Political Writings*, p. 223.

62 Genesis 9:8–9.

63 William Haller, *The Rise of Puritanism; or, The Way to the New Jerusalem as Set Forth in Pulpit and Press from Thomas Cartwright to John Lilburne and John Milton 1570–1643* ([1st pub. 1938] New York: Harper Row, 1957), p. 180.

64 Revelations 3:16.

65 See Stewart, *The Ulster Crisis*, p. 62.

66 See, for example, Seán Cronin, *The McGarrity Papers: Revaluations of the Irish Revolutionary Movement in Ireland and America, 1900–1940* (Tralee: Anvil, 1972), pp 19–26.

67 See H. Montgomery Hyde, *Carson: the Life of Sir Edward Carson, Lord Carson of Duncairn* (London: Heinemann, 1953), pp 365–6.

68 Inglis, *Roger Casement*, p. 245.

69  Pearse, 'From a Hermitage' (November 1913), *Political Writings*, pp 188–9.

70  Dudley Edwards, *Triumph of Failure*, p. 276.

71  Pearse, 'Peace and the Gael', *Political Writings*, p. 217.

72  Quoted in Richard R. Laurence, 'Viennese Literary Intellectuals and the Problem of War and Peace, 1889-1914' in Erika Nielsen (ed.), *Focus on Vienna 1900: Change and Continuity in Literature, Music, Art and Intellectual History* (Houston German Studies No. 4) (Munich: Fink, 1982), p. 14.

73  For these Austrian and other examples, see Laurence, loc. cit., pp 12–22. ['Rough translations' by the author.]

74  Pearse, 'To the Boys of Ireland', *Political Writings*, p. 115.

75  Thomas MacDonagh, 'Barbara: Born 24th March, 1915', *Poetical Works* (Dublin: Talbot Press, 1916), p. 138.

76  Pearse, 'From a Hermitage' (October 1913), *Political Writings*, p. 177.

# Index